Jennifer
Erickson Arts

Author & Photographer

ISBN: 978-0-578-3002-3

Photographs by Jennifer Erickson

Printed In the United States of America

20 21 22 23 24 25 26 27 28 / 9 8 7 6 5 4 3 2 1

DEDICATION

To my partner Steve. You never stop supporting my personal journey. It is our relationship that keeps me from feeling anxious when times are rough. I love you.

TABLE OF CONTENTS

ACKNOWLEDGMENTS

I want to take a moment to thank all the people in my life who have allowed me to help them tackle their anxiety. Seeing people struggle and uncomfortable with themselves has inspired me to keep learning and growing so I can continue to help.

Part 1 – New Information

What does this book help with?

Stop Calling It Anxiety is intended to help you grow, become more confident, and ultimately reduce your overall anxiety. While life will always have ups and downs, having the right tools to adjust and cope can greatly reduce your personal inner discomfort. So, this book offers ideas and techniques for developing coping skills, gaining emotional maturity, and moving through (and eventually accepting) the things in your life that cause you anxiety.

While this book does offer information and help for several different types of anxiety, it is geared towards high-functioning individuals who are not debilitated by their anxiety. Typically, high-functioning anxiety is still very overwhelming and difficult, but it doesn't regularly keep you from working, engaging in social activities, or managing your responsibilities at home.

What isn't included in this book?

This book does help with many types of anxiety, but it is not intended to resolve *all* scenarios or issues. A self-help book can offer a lot of information, but it's not specific to any one individual and it is not meant to be a substitute for counseling or therapy. *Stop Calling It Anxiety* includes a myriad of information, and I hope that you're able to use that information to create significant change in your life, but it may not help with everything you need.

In my private practice as a Licensed Professional Counselor and Health Psychologist, I regularly use the knowledge, techniques, and suggestions in this book. However, working directly with someone isn't quite the same as writing a self-help book, because information and tools can be tailored to that individual's specific anxiety and life struggles.

Additionally, self-help books do not offer professional, step-by-step support as you learn to implement new techniques. So, if you feel you're emotionally healthy enough to tackle your anxiety and its challenges without the direct support of a therapist, I believe this book can help you.

Anxiety recovery is all about actively training your brain and reshaping your response systems, coping skills, and self-confidence, as well as your understanding of yourself, your identity, and the world around you. This means that, to reduce your anxiety, you will have to challenge yourself to practice new ideologies, new coping skills, and allow yourself to see new perspectives.

It's work, and it can be difficult, which is why many people seek face-to-face counseling. Whether you see a therapist or not, please remember that to change, you must do the work. You have to practice, therapist or not. (Additionally, *Stop Calling It Anxiety* can be used in conjunction with professional therapy.)

While this book offers specific suggestions, they can't cover all situations. The goal is to learn these techniques first so you can later adapt them to fit present situations. If you only read a chapter right when you need it, you won't be able to

make permanent change because there would be no reinforcement of the skills. The "doing" is what restructures our personal lens of the world, and our lens determines our emotional and cognitive responses to our lives.

This book also cannot account for other diagnoses you may be struggling with. For example, if you've experienced significant trauma in your life, you may need more than a self-help book to alleviate symptoms and live more freely. If you have biochemical irregularities that cause disorders such as bipolar or schizoaffective disorder, this book won't address everything you're going through. If you struggle with a severe phobia, it may prohibit you from practicing new techniques, and therefore, keep you from experiencing the full benefit of them. This is a self-help book designed for people with mild to moderate anxiety. While I hope it will help you, I suggest seeking further help specifically for any other challenges you're currently facing.

Why should you read this book?

There's an adage that says, "Knowledge is power." The reason I wrote *Stop Calling It Anxiety* is that, in the years I've been working with clients, I've found that to be true--what many people need to make lasting and effective change is information. The purpose of this book is to provide you with the knowledge you need to strengthen your self-confidence, your self-perception, your coping skills, your emotional resilience, and much more.

All that being said, if you understand what this book does and doesn't offer and you're ready to get started on the work it takes to help your anxiety, then let's begin learning.

Chapter One – Gaining Knowledge

The goal for this book is to present you with new knowledge about the brain, personality, and the nuances to behavior change and then introduce you to some skills that can help build confidence, reduce excessive worry, and aid you in finding balance, with the ultimately goal of reducing anxiousness.

This book is designed to help guide people who are generally able to function, who have excessive worry, but can get to work, can participate in life, can be social from time to time.

Knowledge | **Change** | Experience

This book is divided into two parts. Part one is informational; Part two is set up as a self-help workbook. Both parts intent to teach skills that raise self-awareness and self-confidence.

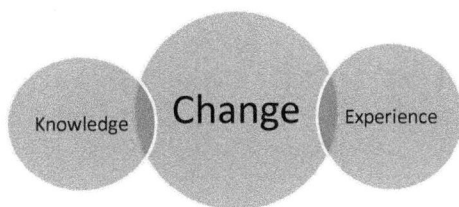

Additionally, the chapters teach life skills such as learning how to set boundaries, how to be mindful, how to understand distorted thinking, understand emotions, and even worldview. Part two also includes some basic information about nutrition, sleep, and the benefits of physical activity. And finally, chapter twelve in part two reviews how to invest in your life.

As you proceed into Part One, it is important to remember that this is a general self-help book. This book does not offer specific medical or mental health advice. It does assume you are in a place where self-help is what you need. Throughout the book, there will be reminders that if you need more than what the book can offer, to seek the advice of a medical or mental health (or other) professional. Information in this book is general and cannot be tailored to fit any one diagnosis or account for any one individual.

Finally, why is this book titled:

Stop Calling It Anxiety

Does it mean that I don't believe anxiety exists? Not at all. Feeling anxious is a true and valid feeling. Anxiety, by definition, is the mind and body's reaction to stressful, dangerous, or unfamiliar situations. Anxiety is the feeling of uneasiness, distress, fear, or dread before a major event.

After a decade of specializing in Anxiety Disorders, what I have found is that the word anxiety can become a person's identity. What I mean by that is, if someone is upset by something a friend, partner, or family member says tend to respond with, "that is just your anxiety". If a person is having a hard time at work, they might tell themself, "That is just my anxiety". If a person is trying to make a change in their life, people might say to them, "your anxiety is too much, you shouldn't push yourself".

Many of these reasons, and more, are why anxiety is becoming a part of our identity.

My definition of anxiety is "the physiological response to excessive worry"

Now, if you don't use the word anxiety, maybe this is what you might say to yourself if you have a difficult time at work.

6

?

"Wow, my body is feeling the effects of the extra workload. I'm so tense and shaky".

Now, if you don't use the word anxiety, maybe this is what you might say if you are trying to make a change in your life.

"I can feel the tension in my body, and I've noticed I'm breathing deeper, and my heart is racing. Maybe I am very nervous about starting this new job (or whatever your life change is).

Now, if you don't use the word anxiety, maybe this is what you might say to your family, friend, or partner if they say you are upset just because of your anxiety.

"Just because I am shaky, crying, nervous, or upset, that doesn't mean what I am telling you is wrong or not valid. I would like you to pay attention to what I'm saying/asking, not how my body is responding".

Do you see what I am saying now? The word anxiety can become our identity, not just a state of mind or body when we use the word too much. That is why it is better to use a more specific vocabulary to describe what is bothering you and how your body is responding.

If I haven't convinced you yet, how about this thought...

Your body responds many times throughout the day. Your heart will race, your breathing will change, you may sweat or feel tense, your muscles may flex in all the following times:

> - Doing yard work
> - Aerobic exercise
> - Strength training
> - Running up a flight of stairs
> - Being in a stressful meeting at work
> - Work itself
> - Walking your dog
> - Cooking or baking
> - And especially during **SEX**

If during each of those events, your physiology is changing, and you are usually aware of it. Then why does your physiology changing during stressful moments bother you so much? I know, that can be a complicated answer, but ponder it a bit. Our body responds often during the day, each day. Don't let its response during stress distract you from the change. And honestly that is what happens when we call it anxiety. We focus more on our body, than we do the stress or the change that needs to happen. And this is where the question of medication comes in. Because this is a very specific and personal question, I can't tell you what to do. Therefore, you may need to speak to your psychologist, therapist, or medical doctor.

What I can say, for anxiety, medication is used sometimes to help our body remain calm consistently. You need to understand if this is the help you need, talk to your doctor or psychiatrist. There are purposes for medication, there are times it is not needed. Weigh the pros and cons and seek advice from your therapist as well. If you are getting on medication and you don't have a therapist, I highly recommend it. I would recommend that if you are seeking support from a psychologist or therapist ask if they have advanced training in anxiety.

As far as other mental health diagnosis and whether medication is beneficial or not, that I can't speak to. That is not my specialty. Again, this book is to help guide people who are generally able to function, who have excessive worry, but can get to work, but can participate in life, but can be social from time to time.

I hope this gives you some basic information about why to Stop Calling It Anxiety. And motivates you to work through all the chapters to learn how to raise your self-awareness and your self-confidence. And get you excited to learn skills about how to take care of yourself and live a health and wellness lifestyle.

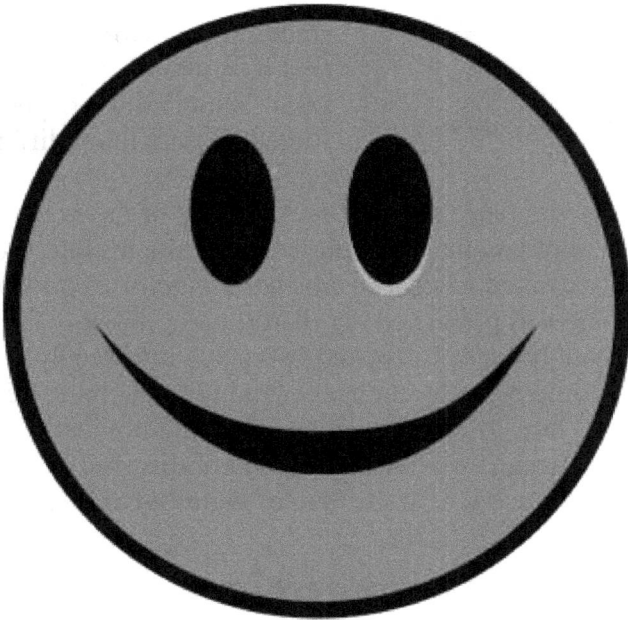

Chapter Two – The Science of Behavior Change

Welcome to the *active* part of this self-help book. I wanted to emphasize the word *active* because change doesn't happen without your involvement and effort.

In psychology, we refer to this as "behavior change," and it's one of my specialties. I have spent a great deal of time researching and studying behavior change because I find it so interesting to delve into what factors motivate people to do something, anything different.

As you read, you will see citations of the experts I reference, but you may also notice that I cite myself, too. I was extremely excited when *The Journal of Social, Behavioral, and Health Sciences* published my dissertation; not only because I wrote it, but because I invested two years into deeply understanding behavioral change, and I love helping people understand how to create such change. And not just change, but the *desire* for change. We'll talk more about this shortly, but first, I want to introduce you to the idea of **behavioral intention.**

Behavioral Intention

The National Institute of Health (n.d.) defines behavioral intention as, a "person's perceived likelihood or subjective probability that he or she will engage in a given behavior." In other words, behavioral intention is a thought process we automatically go through to decide if a certain behavioral change will

happen through certain considerations, such as "Do I intend to engage in this new behavior?" These considerations are rooted in personal concepts such as desire, motivation, and accountability for what may occur if the behavior change is implemented (and for what may not occur if it isn't). Because behavioral intention is the most direct way to predict someone's behavior, areas such as marketing, medical care, and research commonly use behavioral intention to influence their audiences.

Theories of behavioral change date back to the 1950s, beginning with the formation of the health belief model (or HBM). Developed by the U.S. Public Health Services, the HBM is a conceptual framework that helps explain motivation and peoples' willingness to engage in behavior change (Glanz, Rimer, & Viswanath, 2008). It operates on concepts that help us understand motivation. For example: perceived severity, perceived benefit, perceived barriers, and someone's belief in susceptibility. Additionally, the HBM makes use of action triggers to encourage people to change. Finally, it highlights self-efficacy: a person's individual belief in their own ability to change, which is needed not only to change, but also to sustain that change.

Understanding the relationship between intention and behavior is paramount to promoting positive and healthy changes, but I want to focus for a moment on physical activity specifically. In 2013, researchers Rhodes and Dickau performed a study, focusing on the components that increase someone's intention to do physical activity.

Individual variables that influenced the intention to exercise included: intention stability; past behavior and habit; anticipated regret; perceived self-efficacy; planning; cross-behavior conflict; neuroticism; extraversion; openness to experience and agreeableness; and conscientiousness. Environmental variables were limited in prior research, but one consistent variable turned out to be the person's proximity to recreational resources.

In time, the researchers determined that 38 different determinants impact the area of physical activity, but the most impactful turned out to be intention stability.

Intention stability is defined as a person maintaining the same motivational flux or strength over a period of time. People with intention stability can stay motivated in building new behaviors and upholding current ones over time, whereas those lacking intention stability may struggle to maintain the same changes as time goes on. Therefore, results demonstrated a positive link between intention stability and physical activity.

Additionally, Rhodes and Dickau found two secondary factors that often played a role in someone's intention to engage in physical activity: **anticipated regret** *(the regret they may feel if they choose not to exercise)* and **conscientiousness** *(the self-disciplined desire to do a task well and strive for achievement)*.

The strength of Rhodes and Dickau's research proves that we *can* measure behavioral intention, and that campaigns and programs promoting physical activity may be more effective when designed with behavioral intention in mind.

A few years later, Conner, McEachan, Lawton, and Gardner (2016) furthered our understanding of behavioral intention. Within a broad scope of health-related issues, they examined the gap between intention and behavior and how that gap affects motivation, which predicts intention. Prior belief was that someone's thoughts and beliefs shifted their focus to more attitudinal and normative factors--such as whether or not they believed they could succeed--and impacted their likelihood for behavioral change.

> ➤ Additionally, they researched other factors that impacted behavioral intention in health-related changes. They were:
> ➤ anticipated affective reactions *(what we think will happen if we do or do not complete a behavior)*.
> ➤ injunctive norms *(perceived pressure from other people to do the behavior)*.
> ➤ descriptive norms *(how we think others will view us given the completed behavior)*.
> ➤ and moral norms *(whether we believe we have a moral obligation to complete the behavior)*.

In the end, Conner et. al found that, to promote behavioral change in health, anticipated affective reactions were key in influencing intention. So, what we think will happen (or not happen) if we complete the behavioral change is one of the biggest factors in whether or not we change. In fact, the immediate effect of a behavior, whether physical or emotional, is what binds the experience to the person and reinforces the change.

Another group of scientists named Lienemann, Siegel, and Crano (2013) also studied what factors impact behavior intention in a different light--persuading people with depression to seek help but avoiding the boomerang effect of negative stigma.

Depression is a treatable mood disorder that impacts several areas of life. Left untreated, it can increase in severity, and some sufferers become suicidal. The goal was to achieve a balance in promoting behavioral change that wouldn't negatively impact the public through external and internal stigma. Externally, general stigma happens when the public endorses negative stereotypes and prejudices (Grappone, 2018). Internal self-stigma happens when we internalize general stigma, and it plays a large role in decision making.

The hypothesis of this study was that, if they weren't designed appropriately, public service health campaigns could cause an increase in both general and self-stigmas. Leinemann et. al determined this was true; thus, proving that both good and bad effects must be considered in behavioral intention.

Another factor considered in the intention of our behaviors is the behavioral climate. In 2013, Brown, Fry, and Little used the PMCEQ to determine what climate in a gym setting was the most motivational, so exercise leaders could create environments that increased people's motivation to exercise.

There are two categories of motivational climates: task-involving, or ego-involving. In a task-involving climate, we feel that our best efforts are being recognized. But in an ego-involving climate, we feel that only those with superior ability are recognized. This study found that how someone perceives the motivational climate influences how they view their goals.

Additionally, Brown et al. reviewed the Caring Climate Scale, which measures the level to which people feel their fitness center cares about them. In task-involving climates, people usually felt cared for. Those in ego-involving climates felt the opposite. Results were equal for both men and women.

Behavioral Change Theory

After the health belief model, other models continued to further our understanding of behavioral change--one of which was self-determination theory (SDT). Similar to HBM, SDT focuses on how someone interprets and accepts their need to change, and whether they can fully endorse that need (van der Kaap-Deeder et al., 2014).

The SDT operates on the understanding that we only make true, lasting change when we personally accept and endorse it. Without such acceptance and endorsement, we're much less likely to implement changes, and even if we do, the change will only be temporary.

Though SDT and HBM are similar, they differ in that HBM focuses more on what might encourage change--such as perceived barriers and social outcomes of the change.

Meanwhile, Choi, Chung, and Park (2013) have focused their research on a third model: the transtheoretical model, also known as **Stage of Change**. In this model, stages of change are used to explain behavior.

There are five stages of change: precontemplation, contemplation, preparation, action, and maintenance. As people move through each of the progressive stages, they are able to implement and sustain behavioral change. However, those who stay in the precontemplation stage don't realize they need to make a change. It's when practitioners understand these stages of change and how they affect behavior that they can truly help people progress.

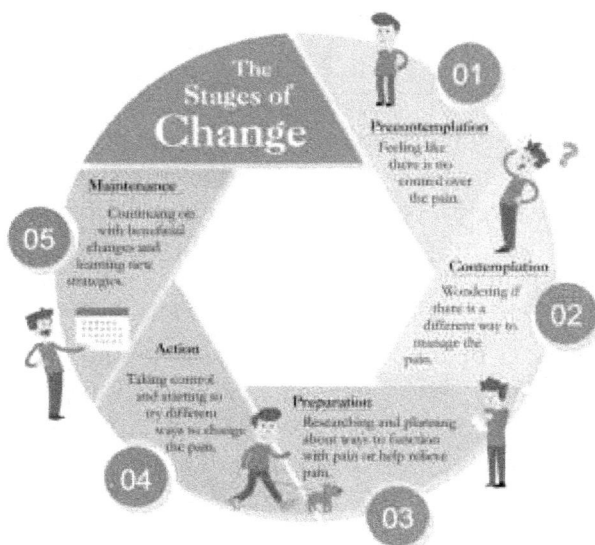

The growth of behavioral change theories led to the theory of planned behavior (TPB), which uses mental cognitions to predict different behavioral beliefs. This frugal theory uses just two predictors: intention and self-efficacy. According to research, intention is affected by an individual's beliefs and attitudes around behaviors, subjective beliefs, and behavioral control. When Hobbs, Dixon, Johnston, and Howie (2013) used TPB to research exercise intention, results indicated that this theory could predict behavior.

However, TPB does have limitations; for example, the closer in time the intention is to the event, the more accurate the TPB's predictions become. Due to the strengths and limitations of behavior change theories in predicting behavioral intention, research continued with a new model.

The Model of Goal Directed Behavior

The model of goal-directed behavior (MGDB) developed from the TPB, and includes the emotion of desire (Esposito, van Bavel, Baranowski, & Duch-Brown, 2016). The inclusion of

desire in behavior change theory incorporates people's wish to do something rather than just their feeling of obligation to do something (Esposito et al., 2016). As a side note, this is my favorite models.

The MGDB uses subjective norms *(perceived social pressure)*, positive anticipated emotions *(desirable consequences)*, and negative anticipated emotions *(undesirable consequences)* to indicate behavioral intention *(the likelihood that a person will engage in a specific behavior change)*. This allows us to measure the perceived effectiveness of any given change (Esposito et al., 2016).

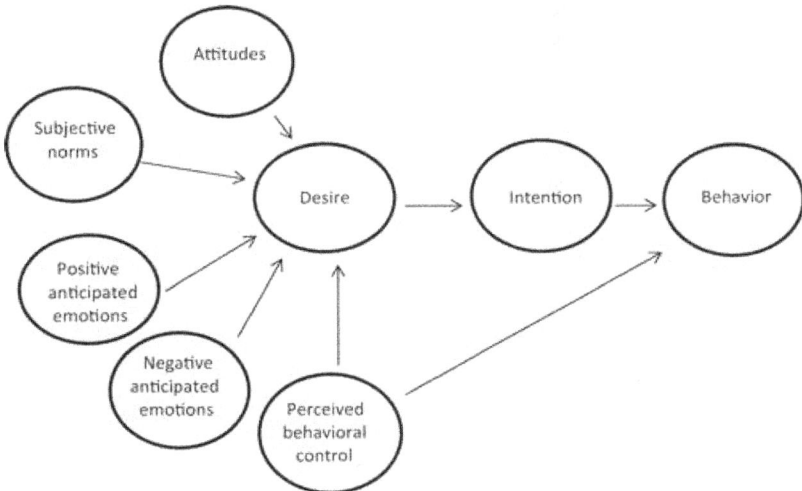

To measure said effectiveness, the study compared the positive and negative affective responses of the participants, as well as how the participants rated the effectiveness of each PSA. Prior research by Bigsby et al. (2013) supports the thought that cognitive and emotional responses can predict whether someone intends to engage in a new behavior, which is also a predictor of perceived effectiveness.

This behavioral change model, previously tested with physical activity, tells us a lot about the intellectual and emotional aspects of how different people process information. Understanding and accounting for how someone processes information is very helpful and informative for researchers, and therefore, it may increase the chance of positive behavioral change.

What does all of this mean for creating change?

People want to feel confident about the decisions we make. We want to trust them and have as little regret as possible. We want to have confidence in ourselves, and we do want the ability to make decisions even when the topic is difficult.

We have learned from this chapter that deciding to create behavior change is a process and it most importantly must include the **desire** for change.

On top of understanding the stages of change, and that we need to understand our desire, we also want to trust our decision make process. This is called the **Decision Making Model**. There are several variations of this model depending on the target of decision making. For our purposes, I'm explaining the basics.

Decision Model Highlights

- ➢ Identify your goal(s)
- ➢ Gather information (different angles)
  - o I tend to suggest 3 different approaches
- ➢ Determine the consequences of each angle
- ➢ Make your decision
- ➢ Evaluation your decision
  - o Stick to 3 sources of information to evaluate from

Effective decision making is a part of life, and we do want to feel good about it. Being able to eb and flow with life is important. For example, if I can only get my food from a restaurant, and I don't have skills in shopping (learning how to tell good produce from overly ripe or bad), learning to read expiration dates, learning how much things cost to get a good value, then what happens in my town has an ice storm one winter and the restaurant is closed, but I can get to the local grocery store.

Decision making is something we all need to learn and feel confident in. Engage in Part Two of this book to gain skills and confidence to grow your decision-making skills.

What I have found throughout my career is that people who struggle with anxiety, tend to struggle with decision making. That "flow chart" that we keep in our mind that helps us make decisions gets stuck or feels incomplete, preventing us from feeling confidence about our decisions.

Do you ever struggle with your decision making??

```
                    ┌──────────────┐
                    │    Start     │
                    └──────┬───────┘
                           │
                           ▼
              NO       ◇ Do I want to do ◇
         ┌─────────────   this?
         │              ◇           ◇
         │                  │
         │                 YES
         ▼                  │
   ┌───────────┐            ▼
   │ Don't Do It│      ◇ Will it likely end ◇    NO
   └───────────┘      ◇  in disaster?   ◇ ─────────┐
         ▲              ◇           ◇              │
         │                  │                      │
         │                 YES                     │
         │                  │                      │
         │  NO              ▼           YES         ▼
         └──────────  ◇ Will it make a ◇ ──────  ┌───────┐
                      ◇  good story    ◇         │ Do It │
                      ◇   anyway?      ◇         └───────┘
```

Chapter Three - An Overview of Anxiety

What is anxiety, and why do we have it?

Anxiety is a natural mental and/or physical response to stress and worry. Although worry is less intense than stress, both are based on fear or apprehension about what is to come. In other words, while there are several different circumstances that can cause anxiety, the resulting worry is future-focused. So, while you may be worried about something from the past, you're typically focused on how it will affect your future. Still, in some cases, anxiety can be focused on the present. For example: "I'm living with someone who struggles with alcoholism." Or, if you struggle with an eating disorder, you may worry about eating *right now.*

As mentioned in chapter 1, if you have other struggles alongside your anxiety, you may need more information and assistance than what a self-help book can provide. So, from this point, I'll be operating on the assumption that you're primarily dealing with low to mid-levels of anxiety (or that if you have severe anxiety, you're using this book as a resource in addition to other help).

Why don't I worry like others?

There will most likely always be a debate on "nature versus nurture." Nature says we are more affected by a given situation due to our DNA, while nurture says we're more affected because of our environment (such as living situation, education, family, social life, etc.). Research shows that there are social reasons why people tend to worry more, but it also supports the theory that biological factors, such as genetics, may play a role. For example, if your family member has anxiety, you may be predisposed to it as well. There is no true way to definitively say one way or the other is more influential. If your parent has anxiety, did they pass it to you through DNA, or did they teach you to worry like they do? As infants, toddlers, and young children, we don't have enough cognitive understanding to question our parents' teachings, so both instances are possible.

Let's talk about the difference between worry, anxiety, and panic:

➤ Worry is a state of uncertainty. In its simplest definition, that's all it is, and it's normal. Everyone experiences it. But worry can become unhealthy if our thinking becomes illogical, and our concern goes beyond trying to protect ourselves. This is when worry typically turns into anxiety.
➤ Anxiety is a psychological state of excessive unease or fear, and it's usually accompanied by a physiological reaction (like rapid heart rate, sweating, muscle tension, etc.).
➤ Panic is the most severe form of anxiety. It's characterized by sudden uncontrollable fear, and it often causes what feels like severe physiological reactions.

Later, we'll revisit these definitions. But first, I want to talk about another factor in how you perceive yourself and the world around you--your personality. Let's dive deeper into how personality can play a role in worry, anxiety, and panic.

How can personality traits impact how you deal with worry, anxiety, and panic?

Good question. I'm going to show you four different personalities--the type A, B, C, and D--and how they may experience anxiety.

Type A Personality: Competitive, overachiever, meets deadlines.

Type As are known to be extremely driven and achievement oriented. They are competitive and can sometimes come across as intense and high-strung. These people set lofty goals and high expectations, then put a big demand on themselves to achieve them.

Because they fear failure, they're very susceptible to stress and worry when it comes to their achievements and success.

Type B Personality: Calm, relaxed, laid back, and flexible.

Type Bs are much more relaxed and laid back than their type A counterparts. However, they can sometimes relax too much and fall into patterns of procrastination. Many type Bs are patient, creative, big-picture thinkers, and can be very people-oriented.

Looming deadlines and unfinished tasks make these people susceptible to anxiety. They also tend to plan too much, so they may worry about the future.

Type C Personality: Detail oriented, not assertive, sacrifices needs or wants, fears criticism.

The type C person is detail-oriented and can be perfectionistic. They generally fear criticism, and they have a habit of suppressing their own emotions.

This personality type is at risk for social anxiety disorder.

Type D Personality: Prone to stress, pessimistic, fear rejection, feels like they're not good enough.

This group of people need care when approached with a stressful situation. They tend to become distressed more easily than others, and their fear of rejection drives them to worry about many things in their lives.

The type D may be at risk for generalized anxiety disorder.

Are you wondering if you're "stuck" with your personality?

The answer is yes--and no. Even though our personality is one of the most unique things about us, it isn't set in stone. While our core personality tends to remain consistent, there are three specific aspects that tend to change as we age: anxiety levels, friendliness, and eagerness for new experiences (Goleman, D, 1987).

From the moment we're born all the way until we die, several things influence our personalities, such as:

> ➢ Birth order, and whether someone is an only child or has siblings
> ➢ Habits (These change and mature with age)
> ➢ Health (Illness, strength, vigor)
> ➢ Responsibilities
> ➢ Personality dimensions (Extraversion, agreeableness, conscientiousness, emotional stability, openness)
> ➢ Personal preference (Can change with age and experience)
> ➢ Level of self-confidence

So, going back to the question above, are you "stuck" with your personality? The answer is, again, both yes and no. You will be influenced throughout your life by different events, knowledge, and experience, but your confidence and self-acceptance will also influence your personality.

Lesson one: don't feel like you are "stuck." Accept who you are, and if there is something you want to improve or change, do it because you want to--not because you feel the need to change for others.

As I mentioned before, our core personality traits--such as introversion or extraversion--usually stay the same, so don't be surprised if you find that some things do remain consistent (Roberts & Mroczek, 2008). But do recognize that personality changes with our self-confidence, self-control, emotional stability, and much more.

Why do I feel like I have more stress than others?

There are generally two reasons. First, you may have a lot of stress in your life externally. Second, your internal view on life may not be objective, and you might be struggling to cope with what's going on.

Reason 1: You really do have too much going on. Too often, people minimize their distress, whether it be from what's happening in their life, their support system, or even the longevity of the stress. We tend to assume that others would probably handle things better.

Reason 2: You struggle to look at life objectively. This is especially common if you're dealing with something new. In foreign situations, we may be less knowledgeable and less confident. Ultimately, this means progress is slower and more difficult, and this increases stress.

No matter what reason you identify with, it may help you to talk to someone who can offer constructive feedback on what's happening in your life, and how you're coping with it. They may be able to offer you some clarity on whether you have too much going on, if there's a new situation, or if you're handling the situation in a healthy way. Effective change requires specific knowledge of what to change and how to change it.

Why does it matter if you really have too much stress or if you just perceive that you do? Because in both cases, excessive stress can have a negative effect on the body and mind. There are many studies that talk about the negative effects of long-term, chronic stress on our physical and mental health:

- ➢ Stress is the reaction to an unexpected event or circumstance. This event is usually different from what we are used to. It is also assumed the event is negative (Contrada, 2011).
- ➢ It is typically the physical reaction of our perception of the event, on the body, that also causes negative feelings or emotions. This is usually referred to as anxiety.
- ➢ Our own body creates the reaction to stress; our sympathetic nervous response enhances the emotional stress factor. This physiological response can be a racing heartbeat, rapid breathing, fast pulse, tunnel hearing or tunnel vision, and raised blood pressure (Laureate Education, Inc., 2012).
- ➢ Many people do not recognize that stress can be caused by physical (medical) change, environmental (natural or man-made) change, and events out of the norm. All these factors go into the level and length of the stress response (Contrada, 2011).

As people work through their stress, they create a natural "flow chart" in their head. They ask themselves questions and try to answer them accurately. It is through this process that the stress response can either reduce or increase, at which point it may reach the point of worry, anxiety, or panic.

What happens though when our thoughts and beliefs aren't balanced? They become distorted. Low self-confidence, low self-acceptance, and/or general fears about "what if" can cause the flow chart in our head to respond in ways that aren't helpful.

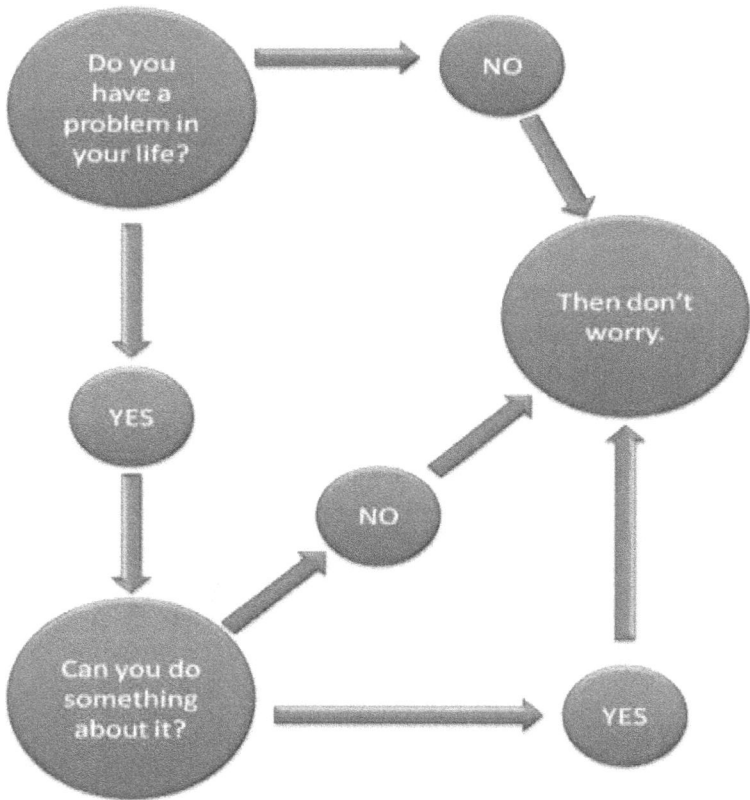

In part two, chapter 1, we'll look at this concept deeper as we review **cognitive distortions** and how they impact our self-concept and our ability to cope with stress and anxiety.

Another factor in understanding anxiety, stress, and coping is resilience: the natural ability to recover quickly from a stressor.

Natural resilience

Again, resilience is a person's natural ability to fully recover from a stressful situation or event. We all have resilience, but the strength of our resilience varies from person to person--and even from stressor to stressor.

For example, one person may not mind working a 10-hour day but may get upset at the sight of a spider. Someone might feel comfortable cooking for a dozen people, while someone else is anxious about cooking for two. But that same person who worries about cooking for two may have no problem driving long distances.

This is the concept of resilience: our ability to bounce back from a given situation, and how quickly we do so. Resilience is influenced by personality and how many stressors someone is dealing with at any given time, along with more influences (Payne, Beth, 2020).

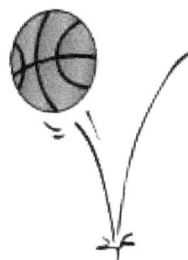

The reality is, we all have situations or events so new or difficult, it's hard for us to bounce back. It's possible for anyone to experience a situation where there are just too many stressors at one time to cope. I encourage you to take some time to reflect on and understand your natural resilience (the things you do bounce back from healthily and quickly) and learn about your personality so you can find solutions that work for you.

For those of you that experience excessive worry, anxiety, and panic--in the next chapter, we'll discuss how you can retrain your brain to strengthen your resilience, raise your self-confidence, and increase your self-acceptance.

Chapter Four - Different Types of Anxiety

So far, we've talked about personality traits, stress, and resilience. Now, it's time to learn about anxiety itself because we can't alter something we don't understand.

Previously, I defined anxiety very generally, as a natural cognitive and physical response to stress or worry. While that definition is true, it's also very simplified. It's time to dig further into the words stress, worry, anxiety, fear, and panic--and then, we can talk about the actual psychological diagnosis of anxiety.

Anxiety is Good!

If you regularly experience high anxiety, you might think I'm crazy for saying this, but anxiety is **good**. There are lots of reasons why fear benefits us:

· It keeps us alert to potential threats, such as illness or injury, for survival and safety

· It helps us plan for future events

· It motivates us

I think we can agree that anxiety has a purpose in our lives. My goal isn't to eliminate your anxiety completely; it's to teach you how to use it effectively, and how to manage it when it becomes ineffective. This is where our next topic comes in.

A key element in most forms of clinical anxiety is that a person's **subjective perception** becomes distorted, rendering him or her unable to discern between a minor problem and a true crisis. A subjective perception is a personal opinion or judgement resulting from a personal experience. This will be discussed more in the chapter on Cognitive Distortions.

But to sum it up, your perceptions play a role in your beliefs, which is why CBT (cognitive behavioral therapy) is so good at helping to reduce anxiety. Through therapy we ask the question, are your subjective perceptions balanced? (Can we see versions of gray or is everything black and white?). Are there difficulties with trouble shooting? How many emotions or feeling words are you using in describing self or situations?

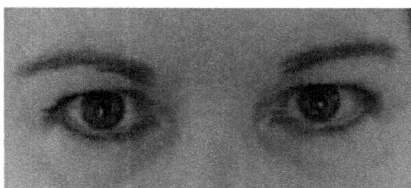

Different Levels of Worry

> **Stress**

Stress is typically any type of change that causes physical, emotional, or psychological strain.

> **Worry**

Worry is uncertainty over actual or potential problems. It represents an attempt to engage in mental problem-solving on an issue whose outcome is uncertain but contains the possibility of one or more negative outcomes.

> **Anxiety**

Anxiety is the mind and body's reaction to stressful, dangerous, or unfamiliar situations. It's the sense of uneasiness, distress, or dread you feel before a significant event. It can also be classified as the physiological response to excessive worry.

➢ Fear

Fear is an unpleasant emotion caused by the belief that someone or something is dangerous, likely to cause pain, or is a threat. The perceived danger, pain or threat could be physical or emotional.

➢ Panic

Panic is the sudden uncontrollable fear or anxiety, often causing wildly unthinking behavior combined with an adrenaline based physiological response.

➢ Generalized Anxiety Disorder

Generalized Anxiety Disorder, also known as GAD, is ongoing excessive worry that is difficult to control and tends to interfere with day-to-day activities personally, professionally, and/or socially. GAD tends to include significant physiological responses that can feel debilitating, even when a medical doctor confirms no physical health conditions.

➢ Social Anxiety

Social anxiety or Social Phobia is a chronic mental condition which causes irrational and excessive worry due to social interaction. A primary component is fear of what others think/the judgment of others, people pleasing, and perfectionism.

➢ Obsessive Compulsive Disorder

Obsessive compulsive disorder or OCD is characterized by obsessions and/or compulsions. It is a condition in which an individual experiences intrusive thoughts, images, or impulses which create a high degree of emotional distress. The obsessions and compulsions significantly impact daily living. You may or may not realize that your obsessions and compulsions are excessive or unreasonable.

➤ Obsessive Compulsive Personality Disorder

Obsessive compulsive personality disorder or OCPD is characterized as a personality disorder, and is defined as a consistent pattern of perfectionism, preoccupation with orderliness, and a pervasive need for mental and interpersonal control. This need for control and sameness often leads to a loss of flexibility and efficiency (The American Psychiatric Association, 2013).

➤ Specific Phobia / Agoraphobia

Agoraphobia is a specific fear of particular places and situations that the person feels anxious or panics, such as open spaces, crowded places and places from which escape seems difficult. Many with agoraphobia have a difficulty leaving their home or neighborhood.

Specific phobia is an extreme or irrational fear of or aversion to something. Both agoraphobia and specific fears can cause a physiological response due to fear/adrenaline response.

➤ Separation Anxiety

Separation anxiety isn't only seen in children. Adults with separation anxiety tend to have extreme fear that bad things will happen to important people in their lives, such as family members. It's often experienced in conjunction with other anxiety-related conditions, such as panic disorder, agoraphobia, and generalized anxiety disorder.

➤ Anxiety Due to a Medical Condition

Anxiety disorder due to a medical condition includes symptoms of intense worry or panic that is directly caused by a physical health problem. It tends to come with a fear of death or dying. In addition, people may struggle with hypervigilance of other "body symptoms" for fear of getting or experiencing "something else."

➤ **Substance/Medication Induced Anxiety**

Anxiety that is induced by substances or medication can be challenging. This disorder is diagnosed when panic attacks or other anxious symptoms are brought on by use of or withdrawal from alcohol or other drugs, taking medications or exposure to heavy metals or toxic substances.

Interestingly, many of the substances that people use to "relax," boost their social confidence or reduce inhibitions in social situations may be the very things that cause this disorder. Rather than providing good feelings or relief, the substance use results in extreme anxiety and panic. Persons with this disorder often don't realize it because they associate their substance use with feeling better, not worse.

➤ **Panic Disorder**

Panic Disorder is typically a condition where you have recurring and regular panic attacks, often for no apparent reason. Many people with panic disorder have the persistent fear of having another panic attack. People with panic disorder frequently go to the hospital or call an ambulance with a complaint of chest pain, fearing that they are dying of a heart attack. They commonly report a sudden unexpected and spontaneous onset of fear or discomfort, with a severe adrenaline (fight or flight) response.

Common Themes of Anxiety or panic disorders

If you haven't noticed it yet anxiety and panic disorders have a couple common themes:

➤ Excessive Worry – many people with anxiety or panic disorders have a skewed response to self, life, events, people, etc. What do I mean by skewed; biased or distorted thinking in a way that is regarded as inaccurate, unfair, or misleading. The real difficulty is that people whose view of events are skewed tend to not realize it, so they often don't have effective communication with family or friends.

➤ Physiological Response – Part of what makes anxiety or panic/phobias so horrible is that they are typically accompanied by an amygdala/adrenaline response. This physical response can be so overwhelming that people focus on this and associate the "anxiety" discomfort as coming from the physical/physiological response and don't realize it can be instigated by their cognition/thinking, with the secondary response being physical.

➤ While there are common themes, I will point out one difference, anxiety tends to be set off by a triggering event, thought or experience, while panic tends to happen randomly (which creates the fear of the panic attack, you don't know when it will happen).

The Biology of Humans and Fear

The reality is humans are full of fear. Researchers are still trying to figure out the function of fear, but when we step outside of psychological research, I think most of us can explain fear and probably even a benefit of fear.

I attended a training hosted by Catherine M. Pittman, Ph.D., HSPP, and she made a comment I loved, "we are the people of worriers." An example of what she meant by that is:

> Image early man, they didn't understand flooding, weather, etc. So, they find a river and set up their village/homes. As seasons change, they end up getting flooded being so close to the river. They begin to worry about it happening again, so they relocate their village. The following year, they worry a bit, it keeps them vigilantly observing the river and how high or low it gets. We needed them to worry because if they didn't, we might not be here today in present times. It is their worry that helped survival.

The point is, worry is not a bad thing. And not only is it not bad, if we don't over-react to it, but rather use it effectively, worry is a good thing. Worry has been a part of humans since early man, but early man wasn't consumed by social media, capitalism, or politics. They were just focused on survival.

I'm glad I live in the present time; however, it means I (and you) have more potential for exaggerated or unconstructive worry. We are now bombarded by social advertising, social media, capitalistic manipulation, political manipulation, and so much more.

Now this might sound negative, and it's not meant to be. It's just a recognition that our present-day time is much more complicated. So, it is even more important to be aware of our thinking, our values, our boundaries, our reactions/over-reactions, and so much more. Luckily, we do have that capacity.

Chapter Five – Understanding Health Psychology

I want to introduce you to my field of study, Health Psychology. I'm sharing this because it has helped me become a more well-rounded person and it is different than just studying counseling or clinical psychology (which is very similar to clinical counseling). Honestly, one is at a master's level, one a doctorate level, and just a few differences in classes.

So, what is Health Psychology? It is the study of how biological, psychological, and social factors affect overall health and wellness. Health Psychologist tend to focus their skills into sub-specialties such as behavioral assessments and testing, behavioral interventions, pain management, illness prevention or acceptance, or healthcare policy (King University Online, 2021).

Health psychology is not well known or understood, but it was started in the 1970s due to the work of Joseph Matarazzo who focused on the intersection of health and psychology. Why is this intersection important? Because it helps people understand that point of deciding (psychological) and understanding the impact on health (physical) and contemplating the potential impact of decision as having a negative impact on the other side.

In fact, Matarazzo believed the amount of money spent on healthcare could be reduced if people were guided to make better decisions regarding their wellbeing, some of the decision people were making that he references were smoking, abuse of alcohol or drugs, excessive use of salt and food high in cholesterol. As of 2016, the Total Annual Health Expenditures in the U.S. had risen to 3.3 trillion dollars or $10,348 per person (King University).

What are the direct factors:

(Both internal and external) in our life that impact emotional and physical health? They are biological, social, and psychological. Let's break that down a little more

> ➢ Biological: Considerations in this area are genetics and biology. This can include age, family history of health, the impact of lifestyle (stress, work hours, eating, exercise, etc.
> ➢ Social: Where and how people live (rural or city, having resources or not, ability to walk vs drive a lot, social connectedness, or isolation, etc.).
> ➢ Psychological: Emotional disorders, resilience, stress level, worldview, etc.

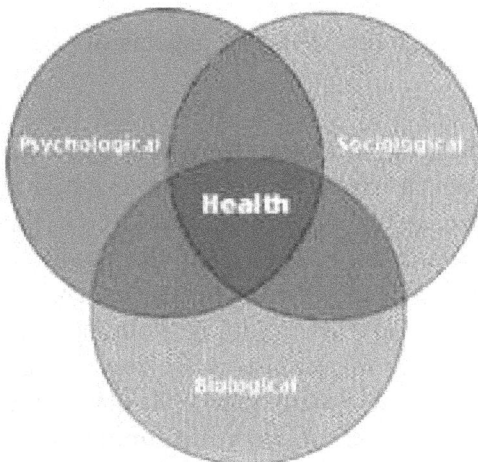

A health psychologist will pay attention to the diversity of an individual's triadic life (biological, social, and psychological) to determine impacts to health and wellness and then conversely, look at the impact of negative or difficult health and wellness issues on biological, social, and psychological aspects.

Long explanation of a health psychologist, but I hope it all makes sense. Now, the more interesting part, the why. Why did I explain all of this? Simple, because I want people to be aware that all the different aspects to our lives, actually do impact our health and wellness. So that job you are miserable at, it is impacting your physical health. And that pain in your back you keep ignoring, it is impacting your mental health (worry, pain tolerance stress). And the decision to move to a new area without a plan of how to connect socially, can cause psychological discomfort (loneliness, isolation) and may even effect social if you need a car and don't have one.

Are you starting to see how our careers, employers, partners, family (extended, parents, and kids), our pets, our city/town, our stress, physical ailments, nutrition, and physical activeness all have an impact on each other? If your goal is to feel better, you must look at all aspects of your life. And be willing to create change possibly, in a few different aspects of your life.

Long story and explanation, but this is why this book contains exercises in many different ways. This book is designed to help you explore cognition/thinking, emotions, your worldview (this could be impacted by culture, generation, region of the country, age, and spirituality or religion), how to set boundaries (interpersonal social and professional interactions), developing your self-worth, self-confidence, and then your groundedness (allowing you to be present with yourself /people, but also with food). It also reviews sleep, nutrition, physical activity/exercise, positive coping skills, and then how to invest in your life.

My advice is to go through each chapter, not because you necessarily have an issue in that area, but because you may learn something that prevents an issue. The goal is to build a lifestyle, not just short-term changes in different areas.

Build a lifestyle of balance, coping skills, and self-awareness. Then the ups and downs (or eb and flow) of life doesn't always have to feel so big. And if perhaps for some reason it is big, you have the personal resilience to go through it.

Chapter Six - How Resilience Play a Role

First, what is resilience. Well, most dictionaries would define it as the capacity to recover quickly from difficulties, your inner toughness. The ability of a substance or object to spring back into shape.

Consider synonyms to resilience:

➢ flexibility
➢ pliability
➢ elasticity
➢ springiness

I love the definition of resilience in relation to engineering or construction: it is the ability to absorb or avoid damage without suffering complete failure. And another: it is the ability to respond, absorb, and adapt to, as well as recover from a disruptive event.

Now how do we put those general definitions into perspective for humans. From an individual perspective we are talking about the concept of capacity that enables some people to thrive and grow despite adversity. From a family or community perspective it is similar. How does a person, a family, or a community thrive and grow in the face of adversity?

I'm keeping this discussion to personal as it is the focus of this book, however, there is a lot of research that goes on regarding the topics of family and communities.

The answer to the question of "how does a person thrive and grow despite adversity? The answer is resilience; the ability to recovery; to bounce back, your inner toughness.

Hopefully, you get the question and answer, and hopefully that leads you to the bigger question.

Do I have Resilience?

The answer is, only you can determine that for yourself. Here is some interesting information though:

- ➢ We can be more or less resilient in different areas
- ➢ Resilience is not based on genetics, but rather perspective
- ➢ Confidence can make us more resilient
- ➢ Personal values can add to our resilience
- ➢ Health and wellness build resilience
- ➢ A proactive view can establish resilience

Before we dig deeper into how to build and maintain resilience, let's talk about what resilience is not.

Resilience is not:

- ➢ Controlling everything or everyone around you
- ➢ Martyrdom (sacrificing yourself for everyone else)
- ➢ Personal strength, or being strong
- ➢ Grit, which is sustained, consistent effort towards a goal
- ➢ Acceptance of toxic or abusive situations
- ➢ Selfish; meaning a resilient person can harm people with low resilience if they are not careful.

Now that you have many definitions of resilience (both what it is and what it is not), let's talk about gaining resilience in a balanced and supportive way.

Gaining Resilience

> **First, resilience comes from experience.** The more experience in an area, the more we can process a difficult situation and recover from it. For example, if you have a flat tire on the interstate, you might already know you can call roadside assistance, you may already be very good at changing a tire, you may already know how to safely move to the side of the road. All your previous experience helps you to prepare for future incidents. This is why some new experiences are harder to bounce back from, while others don't seem to bother us. That being said, when we have a foundation of mindfulness, boundaries, wellness thinking, etc.; then a new experience doesn't always disrupt us.

> **Resilience is not based on genetics, but rather perspective.** You may come from a family of 10, but find you are the only one who sees the silver lining, who sees the different options, or who sees different levels of severity of a situation. Perspective is a personal thing, even within a family. Not all members of a family share the same "thinking," therefore resilience levels can be different.

> **Confidence can make us more resilient.** Now I already talked about experience, but confidence is not just a result of experience. Confidence is also self-efficacy; an individual's belief in their own ability to complete a task or achieve a goal. So self-efficacy is the belief you have in yourself.

> **Personal values can add to our resilience.** Personal values are what a person believes to be important. They help guide decision making. Interestingly many people cannot verbalize their own values, which can be a problem when you are trying to advocate for yourself. This will be discussed throughout this book.

➤ **Health and wellness build resilience**. This is something we are not really taught, and it is not reinforced in the United States. I love this country, however culturally we promote endurance over balance. Endurance is tolerating, and even accepting, unpleasant or difficult processes or situations without giving in. I did not understand this as much until I was traveling abroad for a few months. It is much easier to see our collective behavior objectively when you are not in it. Now, don't get me wrong, I don't want to radically change and be like other countries. For all our flaws and immaturity (remember we are a young country), this is a good country. But culturally we need to continue to grow. I won't get into politics here, but I will say, we need to encourage balance over endurance and perseverance. And before you ask yourself, do I think endurance and perseverance are bad, the answer is no. All qualities are good, it's about balance and in some cases the return on the investment of our time, energy, or skill.

How can I strengthen my resilience?

Don't just learn skills, practice them. Too many times people will go to a coach, a therapist, a pastor, etc. and learn a "coping technique." They really like the technique, in fact so much they use it in that moment, and when the distress is over, they stop.

Later, when another or a new situation comes up because life is never consistent, change always occurs, they have forgotten the technique and go back to feeling distressed. People will ask why that technique didn't help this time. The answer is simple, because for them it wasn't a habit that they could go in and re-access when needed.

Doing something only once or occasionally does not create a habit. Resilience comes from a consistent pattern of behavior or beliefs.

So, if you want to really increase your resilience, then increase your lifestyle skills. Learn how to embrace boundaries, mindfulness, living by your values. Learn how to get physical activity, nutrition, and sleep balanced in your life. Learn to be okay with not knowing everything, and embrace new experience, those will increase your confidence.

Don't get overwhelmed by all the skills, if you really pay attention there are so many things you do every day and you don't even consider them a skill anymore, because it is so natural. This is what health and wellness is all about. And when your body feels good, when your mind feels good, it is much easier to bounce back from adversity.

Just to prove it, think about all the things you can do, that you weren't able to do at 10 years old, at 15 years old, at 18 years old, at 25 years old. Each year you learned new things, you added them to your "skill base" and now they are habits. Health and wellness skills are the same way.

Anxiety can seem crippling, but with a little work, and help, you CAN overcome this

NOTES FROM PART ONE:

_____

_____

_____

_____

_____

_____

_____

_____

_____

_____

_____

_____

_____

Part Two – The Workbook Challenges

Are you ready to start the "active" part of this self-help book? I do specifically point out the word **active** because change doesn't occur without activity, without movement, without involvement by you. Another word for that is **desire**.

If you remember from Part One, Chapter 2, human behavior change requires an intention. I'm hoping after everything you read about in Part One, that you do have intention to make some change in your life, that you have desire. With the minimalistic approach of the exercises in Part Two, the goal is that you will be able to create the change that you are looking for.

Part Two is set up like a workbook, so you can write in the book as you go. This is a nice way to keep all your work organized and in one place. I have arranged the chapters in Part Two in a way that I feel is most effective for personal growth. The chapters begin with the way in which you view yourself and the people around you, and then expand to how you interact with the world and people around you. Popular belief is that you must understand yourself first (inside) before you are able to be more objective and reflective of others (outside). Instead, these chapters are independent lessons in themselves and so you most likely won't have an issue if you bounce around.

"Live the Life of Your Dreams: Be brave enough to live the life of your dreams according to your vision and purpose instead of the expectations and opinions of others."
~ Roy T. Bennett, The Light in the Heart

STOP CALLING IT ANXIETY

At this point, let's stop calling it anxiety. The reason is that some words become labels that we never shake off, and sometimes those people in our life never shake them off. Have you ever been upset, and someone said to you, "don't worry, that is just your anxiety" or "that is a silly way to think, that is just your anxiety," Without meaning to your friends, significant other, family, and even yourself can start to dismiss your thoughts, feelings, and reactions as though they mean nothing.

It's important to recognize that we can pigeonhole ourselves to a state of mind if we are not careful. So going forward, try to refrain from using the word *anxiety*. Through the exercise in Part 2 of the workbook, you will start to learn that we benefit when we react, think, and ponder experiences more accurately. Which means being aware of our inner voice.

Additionally, there are times we may have a physical issue, but we dismiss it as "anxiety." I have met people who will tell me they are anxious, and when we talk about their sleep or eating, they haven't been sleeping and their nutrition is too low to support their energy needs (sometimes hypoglycemic). When they start getting better sleep or improve nutrition, their "shakiness" goes away.

Remember, it is okay to have an anxious moment, but we don't want to get stuck in a label of anxiety. Start to learn your body (when you aren't worried or stressed) so you can tell when your body is uncomfortable and then learn what your body feels like when you are worried or stressed (adrenaline response).

I hope you enjoy the different experiences.

49

Chapter One - Cognitive Distortions

Reviewing **cognitive distortions** is one of the most important steps in self-awareness. Cognitive distortions are exactly what they sound like, "cognition or thinking misrepresentation." It is that inner voice that we hear every day, which helps us make decisions, it helps us respond to events and people, and it encourages or discourages us.

The question is, what would happen if that inner voice was wrong? What happens if that inner voice is skewed and doesn't respond accurately? We could struggle to be able to make effective decisions about ourselves or the world around us.

Let's discuss this. Starting with the term subjective perceptions. What does that mean? **Subjective perceptions** are beliefs based on, or influenced by, personal feelings, tastes, or opinions. Notice the words fact, objective, or provable are not in that sentence.

When a person's **subjective perceptions** become distorted, they can become unable to discern between a minor problem and a true crisis. Having subjective perception is the ability to recognize an **opinion** or **personal judgement** about an experience. We must be able to recognize events or people for what and who they are. We also must be able to recognize our own qualities, desires, and goals for what they are.

We all have subjective perceptions and that is okay, but it is important to recognize that they are personal. An example of this is a roller coaster ride. If we select 10 people to ride this roller coaster, they are all going to have a different opinion about their experience at the end of the ride. Why is that? It is the exact same ride for everyone? Well, some people might prefer the very first car, some the very last, some may prefer more hills, and some may prefer more speed. This is why 10 people who have the exact same experience can have 10 different subjective opinions about the experience.

Again, subjective perception is not a bad thing, but it is important that we are aware that some of our perceptions are very personal and not shared by others. And that is fine. Never try to be a clone of others. Now, what we do need to recognize is that subjective perception can be distorted. Distortion is defined by "altering something out of its true, natural, or original state."

Let's review this. Does having a distorted perception mean that I have a mental health issue. No, not necessarily at all. But it does mean you may be unaware that your perception is farther away from "center" or what the average person might believe. Now I did just say, don't be a clone, but we need to recognize there is some continuity in communities. Such as following the laws, using the Golden Rule, taking turns, etc. There are community standards of treating people fairly and respectfully. We don't want to be a clone of each other, we want to be authentic and individual AND in a way that allows each person to do that (so a shared value of respect). An example of a distorted perception is what we are getting ready to review, aka, Cognitive Distortions.

Let's review the most common Cognitive Distortions. And this is where your first challenge begins. I'll explain the challenge at the end of the chapter.

Catastrophizing

Catastrophizing (ca*tas*tro*fi*zing) is that proverbial, making a mountain out of a mole hill, except worse. Have you had that moment where you called your spouse (or child, friend, etc.) and you know they should be driving home, but they don't answer the phone? And so, you wait a little bit, 10 minutes, and you call again, and they don't answer. And soon, you are wondering if they have been in a car accident. And then you start wondering which part of the road it is most likely they had the accident. And then you wonder if they are dead. Yes, dead. That's it, you lost them. That is where that inner voice takes you.

Does that sound familiar?

It's exhausting isn't it. Many people with anxiety tend to catastrophize, so you are not alone. But that is something that expels too much energy. Afterward you are upset, a 10 out of 10 on a stress scale, and the person you were worrying about is just fine and doesn't understand why you are upset.

So, what is the distortion? The twisting of the facts… is that you did not consider if their cell phone was dead if they did not have a hands-free option and couldn't answer the phone if they were stuck in traffic and didn't chose to touch their phone and even that their phone was in a bag and not accessible. Additionally, there was just no ability to have patience before jumping to the worst conclusion.

Before we talk about the solution, let's talk about the two other cognitive distortions that can go with this type of response, to a lesser degree.

Minimizing and Magnifying

Now, magnifying is pretty much the same as catastrophizing, just to a slightly lesser degree. Using the same scenario, the person you are waiting for that has not arrived yet, you may not think they are dead, but we still image they are hurt, on the way to the hospital, etc. It's still bad and makes you feel physically and emotionally upset when you don't know what is going on with them.

Minimizing is the opposite. Using again the same scenario, the person you are waiting for, well, they are two hours late, but you keep saying to yourself, oh, it's no big deal, they probably stopped, they will eventually get home. That might not sound too bad right, but two hours.

Minimizing can be okay in certain situations. For example, if, like everything, we use it with balance. If you get that bill in the mail for $2500 that is due in two weeks, saying to yourself, "oh, it will be okay, "I'll get to it later", and then we keep putting it off because it is not important. Then minimizing is harmful. However, if you say, "oh, I received this bill, but I'm not going to deal with it today, but I will look at it on Friday," then minimizing is okay. This is because we aren't avoiding, we are just delaying until we have the time to focus on it.

If I had to choose between the three, minimizing has more value in our lives, with balance, than magnifying or catastrophizing. That is, unless there is a Zombie apocalypse, then catastrophizing or magnifying might be useful.

Now, how do we re-balance our thinking to reduce unnecessary and unbalanced responses. Try to image what halfway is... that is more likely the answer. So, the scenario, I'm waiting for someone to come home, but they are 10 min late, catastrophizing would cause us to believe they are in an accident and dead. But what would half of that situation be... maybe they are just stuck in traffic and delayed, and people should not talk or text when driving so they can't tell me. I won't worry until they are 60 minutes late. We counter catastrophizing by rationalizing the facts or cutting the situation in half.

Like catastrophizing, we counter both by rationalizing the facts. We use the "evidence" of the situation.

Fortune Telling

With fortune telling, as humans, we need to be able to predict the future to some degree from time to time. It is the natural ability we develop to predict which outcome is likely given a certain set of circumstances. For instance, predicting that if we drink the expired, foul-smelling milk, we will probably be sick. That is a way of predicting the future. Or when we board a plane headed for San Francisco, we expect that when we get off the plane we will be in San Francisco. To function as an adult, we make these sorts of predictions constantly, and in this way our ability to predict the future is a necessary skill.

Predicting the future becomes a cognitive distortion, when we *assume* that some event or events will end badly for us, that we will fail at something or we will be in danger, more as an *assumption* rather than an educated guess.

What is the evidence for and against your prediction? It is important to examine the actual evidence, and even more importantly, the quality of that evidence. We may be able to come up with lots of reasons that support the fortune telling if we feel particularly bad about it, but would this evidence hold up in court? And consider why it would not be as convincing to someone else.

Examine the benefits of your worry. Are there benefits to making a negative prediction? Does it prepare you for a difficult task? How about costs? Does your prediction instead make you feel powerless or demoralized? Overly anxious? Given the cost-benefit analysis, is your fortune telling more helpful or harmful?

How do we rebalance our thinking? Make sure that you are using an objective way to measure your assumptions. Is your prediction based on education, experience, or training? Find the facts of the situation.

Magical Thinking

Magical thinking, or superstitious thinking, occurs any time that you attribute to an inanimate object, either physical or metaphysical, the ability to shape events. When we use this type of thinking it is as a way to understand that which is not understandable, to control that which feels uncontrollable. We have all heard of baseball players who wear the same pair of socks for weeks or even months because the team has been winning. Someone might own a rabbit's foot, or some other charm believed to bring luck. Have you ever prayed to a higher power in a time of crisis even though you are not particularly religious?

The potential problem with magical or superstitious thinking is it presumes a causal link between one's inner, personal experience and the external physical world. Examples include beliefs that the movement of the sun, moon, and wind or the occurrence of rain can be influenced by one's thoughts or by the manipulation of some type of symbolic representation of these physical phenomena.

Correcting magical thinking is more about feeling you have personal choice and an ability to make some change in your life. Focus on the facts around you, the evidence of a situation, and objective thinking.

Now, I'm not trying to diminish the role that aura, energy, or other metaphysical beliefs, but someone who is trying to balance anxiousness in their life may need to reflect on more concrete belief for a time being.

All or Nothing thinking

When engaging in all-or-nothing thinking, the thoughts tend to go to extremes. An example is "I am either a success or a failure," "my performance was totally good or totally bad," and "if I didn't succeed perfectly, then I failed." This binary way of thinking does not account for shades of gray and can be responsible for a great deal of negative evaluations of yourself and others.

This type of cognitive distortion can derail attempts to create a behavior change because people and events tend to rarely exist in extremes. An example of this is a change in nutrition to manage weight, you might get stuck and not be able to follow your guide perfectly, so then you quit because you already consider it a failure. Or you follow the guide and there is no change in weight after a week, therefore you believe you failed because you perceive it did not work. Basically, anything short of 100% might as well be 0%.

How do we rebalance all or nothing thinking? It is practicing and working on accepting shades of gray. To recognize, "I was thrown off by that one interview question, but the rest of my performance was solid." Or "one brownie doesn't erase the success I've had with my diet. I've made significant changes and can expect things won't *always* go perfectly."

One of the direct challenges I recommend is purchasing finger paints and large paper. Then set your timer for five minutes. Start finger painting and just go with the flow. Many people who engage in perfectionistic or all or nothing thinking tend to struggle with free flow activities, where there are no lines, no order, and no rules. This is why it is such a good practice. I know, it might sound uncomfortable, try it anyway. That is the point, learn to be okay with discomfort. Some other ideas are;

➤ baking lasagna or any dessert that a little messy
➤ put together a gingerbread house
➤ plant some flower seeds
➤ build a house of cards
➤ Lego fun

Remember, anything that has no set rules or expectations. You can't control it; you have to just roll with it.

Mind Reading

Mindreading occurs when a person determines the thoughts and feelings of another person without objective evidence. An example of mindreading is: "I saw my wife raise her eyebrow when I spoke, she must be mad at me."

In this example, there is no proof that the wife was upset just by a physical movement. Interestingly, our brains are predisposed to making connections between thoughts, ideas, actions, emotions, and consequences, whether they are truly connected or not.

Now, to mix in a little more of a challenge, for some people mindreading is a part of their professions. For example, a nurse might have to be observant of someone's look (rosy cheeks due to fever, skin irritation due to rash, etc.). A therapist or counselor has to interpret body behavior. A dentist might notice if a patient grimaces in pain, while they are working, they might check in on their patient. However, if you notice in all the professional examples I used, there is an objective reason for the mindreading.

To reduce and resolve mindreading, we are better off asking ourselves, what is the evidence? What proof do I have that a person is thinking what I think they are thinking? People tend to always assume the worst. To go only by my emotions/feelings or assumptions about the other person means we are not taking in all the information. We may even think, "they didn't respond quickly enough, they must not be happy with me right now," these assumptions can be wrong a lot and they tend to dismiss what else might be really going on. We need to have a fact. For example, if I'm with my boyfriend and he rolls his eyes, why do I assume that he thinks something weird about me. Why can't it mean his eyebrow itches? Or he just had a thought about something he needs

to take care of. And if in the past he did think something weird, was it true? I am quite quirky myself. What he calls weird could just be my unique self. If we mindread negative assumptions about another person, then why be in a relationship. Mindreading keeps us insecure.

The way we stop mind-reading is simple, stop assuming. Stop and ask the question. Say to the person you are talking to, "the look on your face changed after I spoke, what are you thinking?" Let them give you the actual answer.

Personalization

Personalization is the belief that **you** are responsible for events outside of your own control, where you believe that everything others do, say, or feel is a direct reaction because of you. For example, "my husband didn't sleep well last night, I probably kept waking him up." Or when serving dinner, partner asks, "can you pass me the salt", and you think "they probably don't think I'm a good cook, I should have flavored the food better, they are probably miserable eating this food".

A person engaging in personalization may also see themselves as the cause of some unhealthy external event that they were not responsible for. For example, "We were late to the dinner party and *caused* the host to overcook the meal. If I had only pushed my husband to leave on time, this wouldn't have happened."

With personalization, we make everything that happens about us. Now, I'm not going to say that we don't cause others distress, sure. But be specific again, where is the evidence. If you come home and your partner is angry, why assume it is you first? If that is where you go, then we must talk about your self-esteem. Going back to the discussion, this is where you

need the evidence. Ask your partner why they are mad. With anxiety, we tend to be hyper focused on ourselves, and honestly, some family and friends will feel alienated because it isn't always about "us".

Jumping to Conclusions

Jumping to conclusions is a distortion where a person automatically assumes without having the full picture. Similar to mindreading (this is the focus on what someone is thinking), jumping to conclusions is focused more on events or situations. A person jumping to conclusions is basing their reaction, feelings, and emotions on limited information. We assume we know what will happen even before we do it. For example, "I'm not a very good test taker, I'm going to fail this exam." Or "I don't have a lot of experience; I don't think this person is going to hire me" (before job interview). We are traveling in 3 weeks, we might think, "last year when we traveled in August it rained, it will probably rain this trip too. These assumptions take over and we dismiss any other possibilities.

While we do need the ability to assess a situation, we need to be able to step back with more objective and fact/evidence-based thinking, rather than making assumptions.

The way to stop jumping to conclusions, stop and ask yourself:

➢ What evidence are you basing your conclusions on?
➢ Is the evidence complete?
➢ Are you certain or are you guessing?
➢ What other explanations to this situation could there be?

Overgeneralization

Overgeneralization is a way of thinking where you apply one experience and generalize your feelings about it to all experiences, including those in the future. For example, if you once gave a poor speech, you may think to yourself, "I always screw up speeches. I can never speak publicly without messing up."

If you experience overgeneralization, you may view any negative experience that happens as a part of an inevitable pattern of mistakes. With social anxiety, this can impact your life greatly and inhibit your daily routine. Overgeneralization can worsen your thoughts, making you feel that everyone dislikes you and that you can't do anything right.

Reframing is a process where you identify negative or unhelpful thoughts and replace them with positive and empowering ones. It's a way of changing the way you view something. Reframing can be a powerful tool in managing overgeneralizations and social anxiety.

Reframing Highlight

As a side note, some people suggest that reframing is just lying to yourself to make yourself feel better. This is not the case at all. There are very few things in life that are black and white or absolute.

An example might be the weather. One person might see a thunderstorm as scary, cold, dark, where another person sees it as exciting, fun to play in the rain, nurturing, and a great reason for snuggling in at home. Reframing is simply an alternative, but valid, perspective.

It is okay to have a different perspective from others. Don't fear being different. People have different perspectives due to growing up regionally different, due to age/generation, religion, gender, career, talents, beliefs, values, and so much more.

Best example, my children really want something, its very important, and when they must pay for it, they reframe the importance and if they want to spend their money. Perspectives change by themselves all the time. AND we can change them ourselves just by looking at something from a different angle.

Emotional Reasoning

Emotional reasoning is the conscious decision making where a person concludes that their emotional reaction to something defines its reality. Any observed evidence is disregarded or dismissed in favor of the assumed "truth" of their feelings.

To reduce emotional reasoning, we need to review the facts/evidence of the situations. We need to focus on the evidence with a rational mindset, not discarding our emotions, but seeing them as a minor player in our decision making.

One complication that comes with emotional thinking is that if our emotional response developed from a childhood experience, we tend to forget that at 7, 8, 9, 10 years old, etc... that what we believe to be real was viewed through the emotional and cognitive understanding of that age. For example, if you tell a 7-year-old "I'm all tied up and can't help" they might really believe we are tied up. As adults, we need to talk to our own "inner child" and help it realize what it believes to be true was actually distorted due to lack of emotional maturity because of our age at the time of the original experience.

Should Statements

"Should statements" can be tricky. We try to motivate ourselves by saying things like, "I *should* do this", or "I *must* do that"...but such statements can cause us to feel pressured and resentful. Ultimately, we judge ourselves for not doing what we "should" because we believe other people would have done it. We failed.

When you direct "should" statements towards yourself, you can leave yourself feeling like a failure for not doing what you "should." This judgment lingers and can lead to reduced self-acceptance and lower self-confidence.

When you direct "should" statements towards others, you will usually feel frustrated. "He *shouldn't* be so self-centered and thoughtless. He *ought to be* prompt." This type of thinking causes us to feel sour and resentful. "Should" statements generate a lot of unnecessary turmoil in daily life.

To stop... we sometimes need to ask ourselves, "why should I," "who says I should," "what happens if I don't," etc. The goal is to reduce the pressure of the word and make it just an idea to do something, rather than a powerful force that dictates us. Also, when it comes to others, we build relationship health realize when we understand we should not dictate what others "should do". This is reciprocal because we would not want them us how to be or feel.

Disqualifying the Positive

Disqualifying the positive is an extreme form of all-or-nothing thinking in which we filter out all the positive evidence about our performance, and only focus on the negative. It is all-or-nothing thinking, without the "all"! This cognitive distortion will produce automatic thoughts that reinforce negative feelings and explain away positive ones. Someone who is disqualifying the positive can't discuss a subject rationally because they are using a double standard. Negative evidence, no matter how weak or irrelevant, counts. Positive evidence, no matter how strong or persuasive, can be explained away.

To counter this, you want to be fair. You choose to allow yourself to see both the good and the bad. Don't be afraid to take constructive feedback AND enjoy the positive and feel proud of yourself.

An additional thought is, stop for a moment and ask yourself, "who determines what is positive or negative. Many things that you are reviewing are quite subjective. This is why people have such debates and feel differently about events. That is why when someone passes away (depending on why), some people will say that is terrible, we will miss them, but others will say, I'm so glad they are not suffering any more. You can almost say that "events" themselves are neutral. It is each person that assigns the negative or positive association, depending on their worldview.

Cognitive Exercise:

Now that you have reviewed some of the more common cognitive distortions, ask yourself if you see yourself in any. As mentioned before, there are times we may all engage in a distorted though, we might personalize, or mind read. The question is, how often are you thinking this way.

Test yourself for a week. Try to see how many times you can catch yourself having a distorted thought. You can even journal it here.

Monday:

_____

_____

_____

Tuesday:

_____

_____

_____

Wednesday:

_____

_____

_____

Thursday:

_____

_____

_____

Friday:

_____

_____

_____

Saturday:

_____

_____

_____

Sunday:

_____

_____

_____

Now that you have paid attention to your thoughts, did you notice anything? Were you able to make any changes?

Write down your experience so you remember.

_____

_____

_____

_____

_____

_____

_____

_____

_____

_____

_____

Chapter Two – Understanding Feelings and Emotions

Take the time for a moment and see how you answer this question? "How well do you know your feelings/emotions?"

This may seem like an obvious question, but for those of you with anxiety, it may make sense why I am asking.

A lot of people, even without anxiety, aren't always aware of what they are "feeling" or what emotions are being evoked from an experience or thought. This can cause problems because then we might react in a way that is not appropriate, or we might act in a way that is appropriate but someone tells us we are wrong and so we listen to them and not honor our emotions.

Let me give you an example. If you have a beloved pet who passes away, you would most likely be very sad, experiencing loss, grief, loneliness, despair, and so many more emotions. But if you are talking to someone who is not a "pet person" about what you are going through and how you are feeling, you might get unexpected responses.

Someone who is not a pet person might tell you; just go get another pet, then it will be fine, your too old to be upset about a dog, or even why would you cry over losing a cat.

In these scenarios they are invalidating your feeling, not out of maliciousness, but simply because of a difference of perspective. Yes, it would be nice if people could "just understand" each other or show empathy, but the reality is, we are all too different. Just to clarify I did say people don't do this out of maliciousness. I do want to say though, some people do minimize others' feelings, anxiousness, worry, etc. out of maliciousness. Don't assume everyone is just unaware. Again, watch the evidence they provide in their behavior (see the chapter on setting boundaries).

In fact, it is important to recognize that everyone is different, and some people don't get affected by losing a pet, but some of us really do. In these scenarios, if you accept what the other person says as fact, then you may inadvertently deny yourself the need to process your own valid emotions.

The goal with this exercise is to understand your emotions, to look at your feelings, and learn what you feel. Again, this might be difficult for someone with anxiety because people with chronic (daily) anxiety, your prominent word might be anxious, stressed, frustrated, mad, some happy, and sad. But I want to challenge you to find other words. In many scenarios, anxiety is a physical response to excessive worry. So, let's really hone in on what you are feeling.

Remember that emotions are part of human nature. They give us information about what we're experiencing and help us know how to react. This ability is called emotional awareness.

Emotional awareness helps us know what we need and want (or don't want!) and it helps us to build better relationships. This is because being aware of our emotions can help us talk about our feelings more clearly, avoid or resolve conflicts better and move past difficult experiences more easily.

Strengthening emotional awareness happens through experience but when we don't have people in our life who are emotionally strong, we may not get taught the information we need about feelings and emotions.

Lonely

In fact, we may even learn incorrect information leading to emotional dysregulation. A person with emotional dysregulation responds in an emotionally exaggerated manner to these environmental and interpersonal challenges by overreacting: bursts of anger, crying, accusing, passive-aggressive behaviors, or creation of chaos or conflict may ensue.

The personal challenge to help you improve your emotional understanding uses the "Feelings Wheel." Many therapists use this to help people re-identify what they are feeling and experiencing. The goal is to get back to (or start if you never really did) using the correct feeling/emotion word rather than using a generic word like anxiety, fine, okay, sad, or depressed. While they are all legitimate words, many are used generically for 95% of situations. I want you to get more specific. It might be a struggle in the beginning. You might need to look up a definition or two. And there are many more words not on the Feelings Wheel, but that list would be too long to include in the book. Remember the Feelings Wheel has the most common words.

Awful

Emotion Exercise:

It's time for the exercise. This will last for 7 days, and I recommend trying to do it all 7 days. The reason for really trying to do all 7 days is to get as much information as you can about your thinking. The worksheets have 9 days just in case you want to go longer.

Instructions: Each day you will check in with yourself, and ask yourself, "How am I feeling?" You will do this three times a day. Breakfast, lunch, and dinner make it easy to remember. At each check in use the feelings wheel as a guide and pick 3 feeling/emotion words to help articulate how you are feeling. Write down the three words, and next to each word, explain that word so you remember why you selected it. You can use a feeling/emotion word that is not on the list, the feeling wheel is just to help.

Day 1

Breakfast:

_____   _____

_____   _____

_____   _____

Lunch:

_____   _____

_____   _____

_____   _____

Dinner:

_____   _____

_____   _____

_____   _____

Day 2

Breakfast:

_____   _____

_____   _____

_____   _____

Lunch:

_____   _____

_____   _____

_____   _____

Dinner:

_____   _____

_____   _____

_____   _____

Day 3

Breakfast:

_____ _____

_____ _____

_____ _____

Lunch:

_____ _____

_____ _____

_____ _____

Dinner:

_____ _____

_____ _____

_____ _____

Day 4

Breakfast:

_____ _____

_____ _____

_____ _____

Lunch:

_____ _____

_____ _____

_____ _____

Dinner:

_____ _____

_____ _____

_____ _____

Day 5

Breakfast:

_____ _____

_____ _____

_____ _____

Lunch:

_____ _____

_____ _____

_____ _____

Dinner:

_____   _____

_____   _____

_____   _____

Day 6

Breakfast:

_____   _____

_____   _____

_____   _____

Lunch:

_____   _____

_____   _____

_____   _____

Dinner:

_____   _____

_____   _____

_____   _____

Day 7

Breakfast:

_____   _____

_____   _____

_____   _____

Lunch:

_____   _____

_____   _____

_____   _____

Dinner:

_____   _____

_____   _____

_____   _____

Day 8

Breakfast:

_____   _____

_____   _____

_____   _____

Lunch:

_____ _____

_____ _____

_____ _____

Dinner:

_____ _____

_____ _____

_____ _____

Day 9

Breakfast:

_____ _____

_____ _____

_____ _____

Lunch:

_____ _____

_____ _____

_____ _____

Dinner:

_____ _____

_____ _____

_____ _____

Let's review…

Did you notice any patterns?

_____

_____

_____

_____

_____

_____

_____

_____

_____

_____

_____

_____

Some patterns might be more negative then neutral or positive word choices. Similar feeling at the same time of the day. Recognizing word choices that are more exaggerated than they need to be or the reverse, that your usual choice would have been more exaggerated than it needed to be.

Did you find new words that are more specific, but you didn't realize before. Describe below:

_____

_____

_____

_____

_____

_____

_____

_____

_____

_____

The goal from this exercise is to make you more self-aware, because without being able to articulate to yourself what you are feeling or experiencing, how can you share it with others.

How can you communicate and set boundaries, if you aren't sure what you are trying to say?

This exercise is not meant to solve the problem, rather just help you identify any repeating patterns that you might need to reinforce (if they are positive) or change (if they are negative).

If the other exercises don't help you make this change, this is a good time to consider if you need to be talking to a therapist for a few weeks to help you get your emotions more in check.

Chapter Three - Worldview

One's perception of the world around them is important. It is important because it guides our decision making. Now, when I say worldview, I don't really mean the whole world, but rather our core philosophy of life or conception of the world. The foundation of our worldview is our moral compass and our values. It is the driving force behind many of our decisions.

Why is understanding worldview important and how does it affect my worry? Simply because you may see a person as smarter, not as experienced, too different to understand, etc. Or they may see you or your feelings/opinions/actions as incorrect. If we are often being told we are incorrect, we might believe it. That is why we need to understand our worldview or the other persons worldview.

An example of worldview. I am from Minnesota. It gets very very, extremely very cold there in the wintertime. In fact, many days/weeks are -32 degrees (not including wind chill). Yes, that is a minus in front of the 32. So, when I moved to Florida and people complained about the cold at 40 degrees, I probably raised my eyebrow. Yes, slightly in judgment, but not disrespectfully. But I am from Minnesota. It doesn't mean that someone in Florida is not cold at 40 degrees. Of course not. When you have temps 95+ for many weeks in the summer, 40 degrees is very cold.

This is why understanding your worldview, or the other persons worldview is so important. Because two people can have a very different understanding and still both be correct.

The question is:

How do I know if my worldview is accurate?

And if it's not accurate, how do I know that too?

And finally, what if my worldview is significantly different from others? How would I know?   It can get overwhelming.

Let's start with the last part, "what if my worldview is significantly different from others?" I discuss this in a lot of couples counseling session or with parents and their adult children. Many times, a person will ask me how to help them get their family, parent, adult child, or their partner to understand and accept their worldview, to almost agree to it.

This actually leads to the first part, before we try to convince someone that our worldview is the best or more accurate, the question is, "how do we even know if our worldview is accurate? Could it be possible that our perception is actually distorted? The answer is yes. The difficult thing is knowing it and determining what our belief is if we are just different from our social group or culture or if there is something inherently wrong in our thinking.

I think the way to decide is to go back to the foundational things we have discussed, your boundaries, your self-esteem, and any cognitive distortions. If you feel you are seeing the world and life, in a well-rounded healthy way, then you are good. It could still mean that you see it different than your own culture.

For example, a woman who does not want to get married and have children and does want to focus on her career. Depending on which country, community, or family she grew up in, this could be no big deal, or it could be terrible. Does it mean she is wrong? No, if she is comfortable with her choice, then she is just different than her community. Does it mean that people may not understand her and want her to fit in to the "norm," sure. And it's important to know she doesn't have to.

When I talk to people on the journey to figure out or confirm their worldview, I ask them; "How do you know you like something, dislike something, or believe in something?" Is it because you were told to, or because you actually had the experience and have the facts to make a decision? Now, this might even go with faith in some ways, but I'm going to stay away from the religion topic. It would require writing too many variables. But this is where you could go to your Priest, Pastor, Rabbi, Minister, etc. and speak to them. Find out what you feel good about, what you don't, and where you can learn more.

Let's assume you feel comfortable with your worldview.

You feel like you have a set of characteristics you believe in and try living up to. Maybe you try to do a good deed daily. Maybe you try to respect your elders. Maybe you believe in the golden rule. Whatever you have figured out for you, you do try to live by it. And for example, within your belief system, you feel that volunteering is a part of your life. It means something to you to give of your time, it also makes you feel connected to others. And you enjoy the activities. You feel good about yourself.

A difficulty can occur when your family or partner doesn't understand, accept, or agree with your worldview. It is important to talk through this, and the use of a coach, pastor, or therapist can help. Although most of the time professionals help your family or partner by helping them to accept your worldview. Coaches, pastors, therapist really don't help people change to please another, but rather we help the other person accept your worldview.

So, why can't I help someone understand another person's worldview?

And why can't I help someone to agree to another person's worldview?

Let's pause for a moment to consider the questions.

~ PAUSE ~

Some of the reasons why, well, to understand someone's worldview typically you need to have had a similar experience as the person. Even siblings might not totally understand each other's worldview. They might have had the same parents, but most of the time (except for twins), the parents are at a different age when they have their first born as compared to when they have their second, third, or so on. And parents' viewpoints on raising children may change from first born and then with each additional child. Also, do the parents use a day care sitter or babysitter, or some other person involved in the raising of the children. And did each child get the same experience. So, hopefully this shows that siblings don't really get the same parent experience. And then of course, there is school, different classes, different teachers, different classmates, or peers. Different life or world events that happen.

Hopefully you can see, if siblings can have different worldviews, then it is almost impossible for two people who meet to have the same worldview. Two people who randomly meet will have two totally different life experiences. If we don't live life the same way, then it is hard to understand the others point of view. We can understand at a very high level, cognitively, but rarely emotionally.

And if we can't understand it, then how do we come to agree to something we don't understand. In fact, this kind of goes against other topics I have been talking about such as being authentic, understanding yourself through your experiences, etc.

So, in relationships, in families, etc., the goal is to **accept** that someone has a different worldview than us, and that it is okay. In a relationship, the goal is to ask yourself how you can help your partner fulfill their needs. What is in their boundary, while respecting your differences. You accept those, while at the same time not compromising our own boundaries.

Worldview Exercise:

Try this to help "accept" another person's worldview (or call it perspective). Just ask yourself, if their worldview is to volunteer at a facility on Christmas Eve, does that take anything away from my boundary or my worldview. If not, wish them well.

Remember, you don't have to join them, because it is their worldview. You can though, if you want, to share in the experience with them.

But let's say it may cross your boundary (chapter four we review this). Inside your circle is "family quality time." Then do you need to break it down. Is your partner volunteering too much? Are they asking for this one special day? Do you already have a lot of family quality time? Ask these questions and then discuss how to meet both needs. Where is the balance between what each person needs?

Write it out, brainstorm it, but try to figure it out rather than giving up and just say, "find, do what you want." That will just build resentment.

Now, let's get to the exercise:

On the next page is a Worldview Worksheet. The V represents your worldview. At the point (at the bottom) the space is very narrow because you only know what your parents/family have been teaching you. And then, as the V opens, your worldview expands.

Write down all those people who most influenced you up until graduation. It could be parents, teachers, coaches, classmates, grandparents, job supervisor, pastor, or more.

Then write down all the people who influenced you after high school. It could be college professors, job mentors/trainers, bosses, friends, group members, and even famous people who you have come to learn something from.

To the left, it is the decades timeline. Write down any significant world or life events that might have had an impact on you. For example, 9/11, a favorite actor passes away, space mission, a city/state tragedy, or more.

This gives you an idea of many of the people and events that have changed your worldview. There are most indicators as well, are you a Northerner, Southerner, from the East Coast or West Coast. Different regions have different norms or customs. Additionally, religion, race, culture, gender, and so many more difference impacts our worldview.

Now, even more importantly, if you want to understand how differently you are from your partner, have them complete this as well and then talk about how you each developed certain points of view or beliefs. This will be a great conversation.

Your Worldview

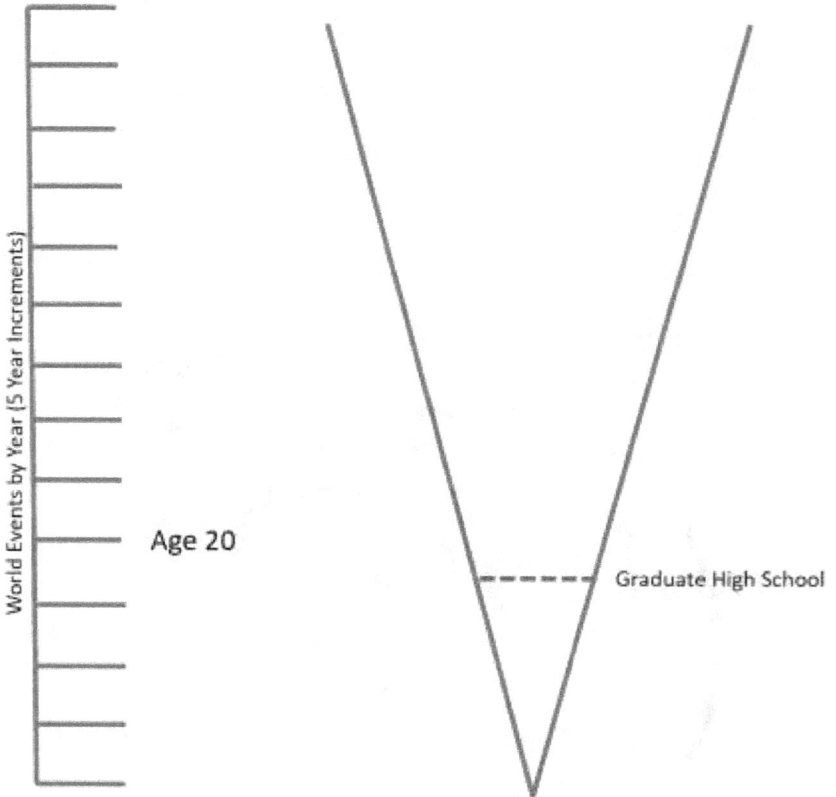

World Events by Year (5 Year Increments)

Age 20

Graduate High School

Your Partner's Worldview

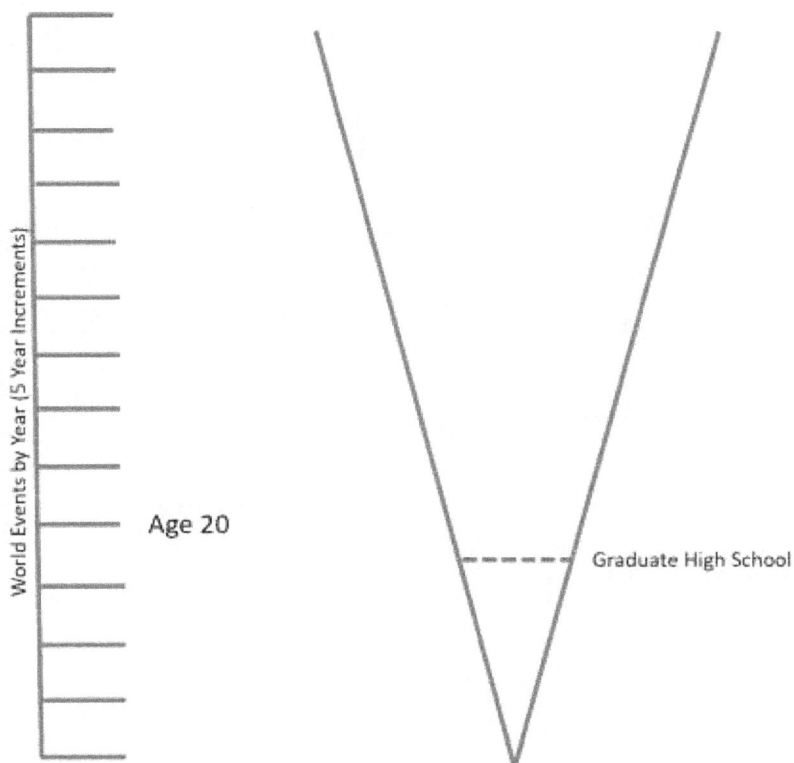

World Events by Year (5 Year Increments)

Age 20

Graduate High School

Chapter Four - Setting Boundaries

Our emotional and relational boundary is no different than a physical boundary we might put around our home, like a fence. The goal is to keep the good things in and the bad things out. Of course, emotional and relationship boundaries are not quite so clear all the time. That is why this exercise is so helpful.

This exercise is an opportunity to explore who you are as a person, what are your wants, and what are the things you don't want in your life. There is an area I call "neutral," and I'll explain that in a minute.

Now, one side note. Remember as you do this, everyone has boundaries, so once you figure out yours, it is important to recognize that we all have them (or should) and it's about balancing different boundaries in relationships. We will talk about that at the end of this chapter.

How well do you know yourself?

That is one of the toughest questions I ask any client. Over the years I have seen many reactions to this exercise. I have seen tears, fear, and just plain confusion. The reality is, we should have boundaries. We should know what we are willing to accept from all people and things in our life. Some people will tell me, "I'm a mother or a father, and now my life is theirs. Or "I'm caring for my elderly parent, and now that is my primary focus." Even better yet, "I love my partner/spouse so much, I want to show them by focusing on them."

What do you think happens to people when they spend 95% of their time focusing on someone else? I hope you guessed. The answer is, they begin to lose themselves. What started as a caring gesture, has turned into a self-imposed restrictive life. Over time, the person who is giving of themselves too much can become aware that other people get what they want, the giving person may begin to realize they aren't getting anything they want and may begin to feel resentful. Sadly, many people then start to feel guilty, because they are feeling resentful or burned out on the other person's life. And the difficulty is, they created this whole situation by giving too much.

Self-Care Highlight

Self-care is not selfish, it is not narcissistic, it is not arrogant, it is not egotistical.

It means you are doing things to take care of your mind, body, and soul by engaging in activities that promote health and wellness living and reduce stress.

Engaging in self-care enhances our ability to live fully, vibrantly, and effectively. The practice of self-care also reminds both you and others that **your needs** are **valid** and a **priority**.

So, let's talk about this.

How do you have a healthy balance between self-care and "others-care." Therapists enjoy using an airline term; the "oxygen rule." During the pre-flight safety talk, the flight attendant will tell everyone, if the oxygen mask comes down, put yours on first, then help children or others. Why? It is simple; if we don't have oxygen, then we'll collapse and then we won't be in the state of mind or body, to help others. These other people you've dedicated so much time to.

The life rule is... Put your own oxygen mask on

first. Take care of yourself. Live your life. Be confident. Assert your needs, respectfully. And then help others with the extra energy you do have.

> "The perfect man of old looked
> after himself first before looking
> to help others" ~ Chuang Tzu

Now it is time to figure you out, hence the need for the boundary circle, but let me talk to parents for a moment.

I read a book when my daughter was around a year and a half old. It was inspiring and I wish I could refer it, I don't remember the title, but I'll never forget the advice of the author. Let the center of the world revolve around your child until they are

2 years old, but then, start to teach them they are not the center. That they have to wait, to share, to be patience, and to adapt to others and events. And then around 10 (remember double digits), start preparing them for high school and adult life.

Now, that doesn't mean tell them to get a job and buy their own toys, but yes, it does mean, have them clean their own room, have them wash their own clothes, have them commit to a chore. All these things will prepare them for life after YOU. And that is a good thing.

In working on your Boundary Circle, if you have children under 2, you may list your child in your boundary circle, because part of your time is theirs. BUT, if you have a child over 2, you cannot list them. Now, I'm not implying they are not important to you, but it is okay to think of life without them. It is a given that they are very important to you.

As a therapist I learned this exception the hard way. Before I set this exception about children, I would tell people to list "what is important to them" and many who are parents would list their parents, their children, and their spouse. Now, not sure if you are following me or not, but that totally misses the whole, "getting to know you" aspect of this exercise.

Rules for Boundary Exercise

Again, if you have children under 2 list them, if they are over 2, then don't list them. Also, no listing partners / spouses, parents, or other family members. What you can list is "family." That includes everyone. I know, it might not seem fair, but we didn't start on this journey to be fair, we started on it to get to know YOU!

Focusing our boundary items; These are things that you want or don't want in your life. These things can be tangible or intangible. For example, spirituality is intangible and getting nails done is tangible. The goal is to come up with at least 6 – 10 items both inside the circle and outside the circle (see next page)

If you are having a hard time thinking about your items, image that the world is empty of people and there are no restrictions, and you can do anything you want.
Now don't worry, everyone will come back in a couple days. Maybe they are hanging with the aliens for a bit.

Here is your worksheet. Feel free to write on this page or draw this out on a separate piece of paper.

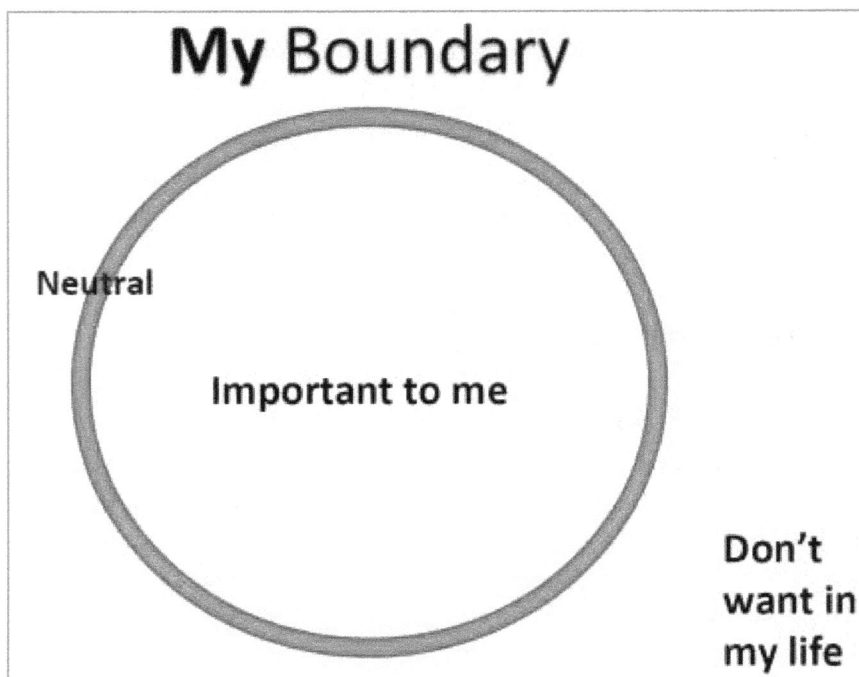

My Boundary

Neutral

Important to me

Don't want in my life

Take the time to think about this for a few minutes. It may even take you a few days to ponder your choices of what is really important and then what is really important to not have.

~ Pause ~

While you are pondering, I'll explain the neutral items. These are things some might ask you to bring into your life, but they don't go against your boundary.

Neutral Items

An example: you have a boundary that is "quiet time." And your friend asks, "would you mind watching my dog on Friday?" And you don't have anything against dogs. You can call this a neutral item. It's something that someone is asking you to incorporate into your life, for a short time, but it doesn't take away from your life, or bring into your life something you don't want.

Now, let's say this dog is a hyper, but loveable border collie. No offense to the border collie, but they need some action time. If watching a friend's border collie disrupts needed "quiet time" for you. **Do you say yes?** Maybe, maybe not. You might need to consider whether this would bring anything into your life that you don't want (busy time vs quiet time). I'm not going to give you the answer, that is personal, but hopefully you can see where I am going.

We need to think through our decisions.

If I say yes to everything, especially with the intention of helping and being nice, and then I bring something into my life that makes me upset and/or prevents me from getting what I need in my life, that is a negative decision.

Have you heard the saying, "**I am my own worst enemy**"? Well, now you see where it comes from. Sometimes **we create** or allow others to create disharmony in our lives. The goal is to find balance. To promote what makes me happy and healthy, and to keep away, what doesn't.

Boundary Exercise:

Okay, you've had time to think. Can you come up with your 6 – 10 items inside your circle, and outside your circle?

How are you doing?

If it helps, I will show you my boundary circle.

My Boundary

Mistrust

Neutral - Jeep "things"

Unethical people

Physical activity and healthy foods

Someone to not accept me "as is"

Neutral

Connection to my family

Socialize with friends

To be "home" poor

Financial stability

Important to me

Minnesota Vikings

Non-reciprocal relationships

Photography

Financial stress

Volunteerism

My career

To be tied to my career too much

Travel and fun

Don't want in my life

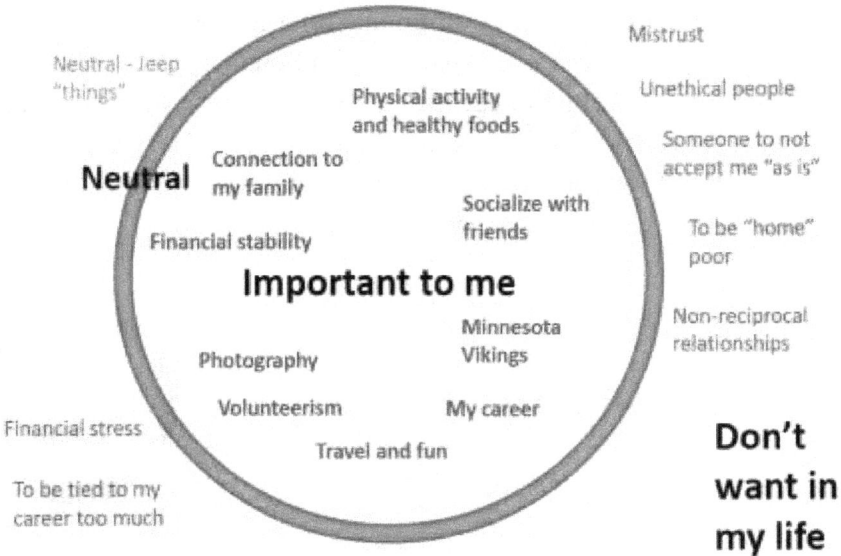

I created my boundary to demonstrate what I am talking about. Yes, this is actually my boundary. My children are college age, so you can see I just made an entry for "connection to my family." This also includes my mother, my boyfriend, his mother, and cousins.

My neutral item, which is from my

boyfriend. He is a Jeep person. For fun we go to Jeep events. I don't mind, in my boundary I do have "travel and fun". And there is nothing in my "don't want" that would suggest this is a bad thing. Now, the reason it is a neutral item and not in my boundary, is because it is not MY thing. It is his. I need to make sure I spend most of my energy focusing on my needs and being authentic.

I hope you are not gasping as I say, "I have to make sure I spend a majority of my energy focusing on my needs." It is not a bad thing. It doesn't mean I don't make time for the important people in my life, remember, that is also a boundary item. But it does mean it is not selfish, egotistical, or narcissistic of me to focus on me. It is healthy. For some reason, our country really pushes this idea that if we don't focus on others, and make others happy, then we are narcissistic, arrogant, selfish, etc.

This is very incorrect.

Let's play a game as we develop our boundaries.

What is something that I might be bringing into **my own life** that directly contradicts something that is important to me?

*** time to ponder***

Are you ready? This is where we hold ourselves accountable.

How about "financial stress"?

If I travel and have too much fun, I might rack up the credit cards. Or if I buy that $5000 camera I want, that could do it too.

In my boundary I don't want **financial stress** in my life AND **financial stability** is important to me.

This demonstration shows I do have to be careful I'm not bringing this imbalance **into my life myself** or letting others, for example, my college age children, bring this into my life. I have this type of control.

What do you think about your boundaries now?

Do you need a few days to work on them? That is okay. It can take several days to really think deeply about what is truly important to us and what we truly don't want in our lives.

In fact, I think it is a healthy thing to review our boundaries every year, maybe New Years, maybe on our Birthday. You pick, but it is good to sit and reflect for a bit.

Go ahead and take a few days to think about them. Even put the book down for a couple days and come back to it. This is important and we don't want to rush answers.

Pause day 1 – take a break from learning

Pause day 2 – take time to self-reflect

Pause day 3 – do something fun today

Have you taken a few days off from "learning" and to live, allowing yourself space to think about your boundaries? I hope as you were pausing, you thought about your boundaries and continued to add to your circle. Now let's learn how boundaries work in a relationship.

Boundary and Relationships

Now, let's talk about boundaries and relationships. The below image shows what the blending of boundaries might look like in a relationship:

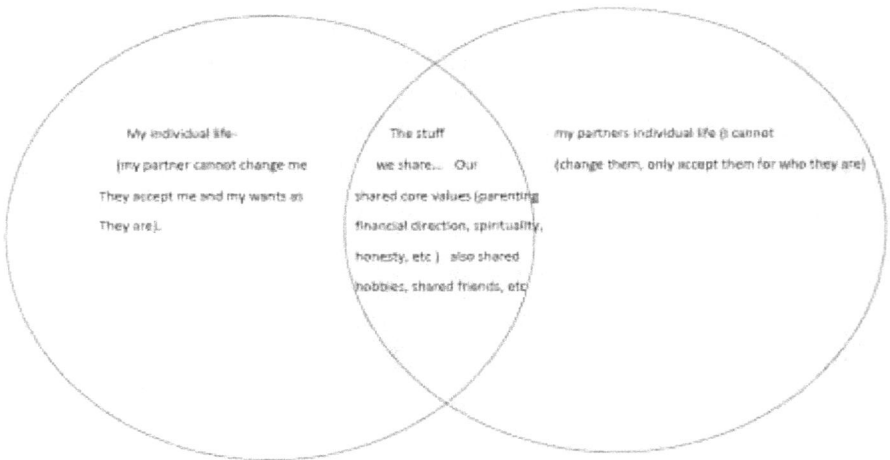

You can see our circles (or ovals if you are type A), overlap, but only a bit. And this amount can vary, but it's never a total overlap.

Core Values in Relationships

In the overlap (from the diagram on previous page), these are our shared values. Typically, they are what we call core values. They are the values that ground us or are foundational in our life. They might include faith or religious beliefs, financial beliefs, parenting beliefs, health stability beliefs, and there are many more (and they can be unique to individuals, such as volunteering beliefs). These don't all have to be the same, but they tend to be close or totally accepted by the other.

The rest of the circle is still our own thing, focusing on our own personal needs. The core values are the foundation that tend to hold the relationship together. These are the things that when he leaves his shoes in the middle of the room and you trip over then, you think, okay, but at least we are on the same page for retirement. Yes, it does mean we need to learn how to live together and share a space, but those are the little details. Fundamentally it helps if we share core values.

Core Values Highlight

Let me ask, do you know what your top 5 core values are? This is the time to stop and think about that.

We need a strong "**why**" in order to support our own change.

It is very likely that your underlying values prompted you to seek help. Maybe it was even the physical exhaustion of "anxiety". We'll be reviewing this again in Part 2, Chapter 12.

Authenticity	Friendship	Nature
Adventure	Family	Perfection
Achievement	Freedom	Power
Acceptance	Gratitude	Punctuality
Appreciation	Generosity	Perseverance
Accountability	Honesty	Purpose/meaning
Compassion	Health	Recognition
Commitment	Helping others	Respect
Competence	Humor	Status
Community	Independence	Success
Connection to others	Intelligence	Spirituality /Religion
Career	Intimacy	Solitude
Creativity	Integrity	Serenity/inner peace
Discipline	Joy	Security
Discovery	Justice	Trust
Education	Knowledge	Tolerance
Equality	Love	Variety
Faith	Loyalty	Wealthy
Fun	Leadership	Wisdom

Write down your top 10 values

Value Number　　　　　　　　**Value word**

_____　　_____

_____　　_____

_____　　_____

_____　　_____

_____　　_____

_____　　_____

_____　　_____

_____　　_____

_____　　_____

_____　　_____

When we are dating, I define dating as

taking time to get to know each other, also known as courting, there will come a time we share our "important to us" items, and we need to ensure that the person we are dating is okay with cheerleading for us, supporting us, and wishing us the best in achieving what is important. This is reciprocal as well; we do the same for them.

That is a healthy relationship in that we have common goals and values, but we each have our own. We don't ask the other person to give them up, forget them, sacrifice them for us, etc. We are happy to see our partner achieve their dreams and goals.

Any time we are in a relationship where our partner minimizes our goals, wishes, wants, then we might need to consider what the future might look like over years. When people support the other, there is respect, confidence, security in that relationship. Don't let go of what is important to you and don't settle and let someone bring things into your life that you don't want.

Keep your standards high, AND realistic. You will probably find a great partner.

Now, what if in a relationship our circles are mostly or completely overlapped?

Then you might have to ask yourself, am I in a **codependent relationship**. A codependent relationship is one where one person relies on the other for meeting their emotional needs. Some, but not all, codependent relationships can become emotionally destructive or abusive. We won't go into this a lot here, but this is why having clear personal boundaries are so important.

If you feel your relationship may be destructive or abusive, please reach out to a coach, faith leader/pastor, or a therapist. Or call the **National Domestic Violence Hotline – 800-799-7233**.

What happens if you live your life supporting the other person, this could even be your children.

What happens to you? Your circle becomes enmeshed with theirs. You are now living their life, helping them to feel better, helping them to achieve their goals. But where does it stop?

Codependent Boundaries

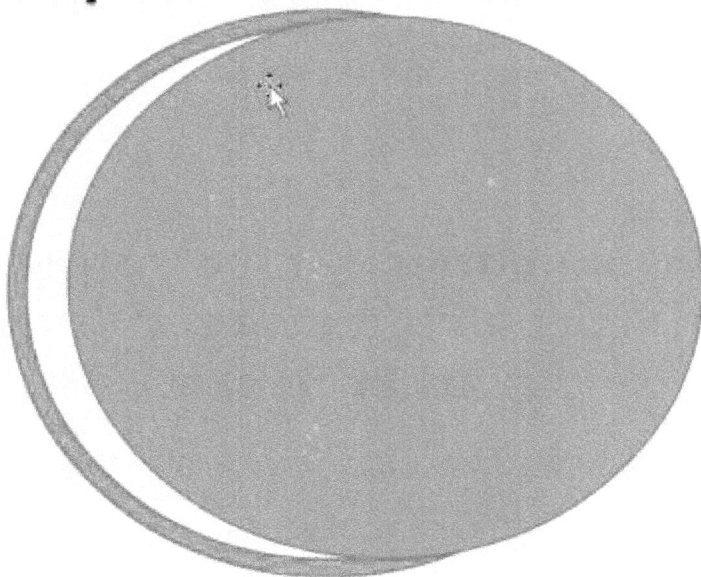

The question is, why do you stay in this type of relationship? Or at least, why do you not separate and start setting firm boundaries. Are you afraid to live on your own, are you not sure you can reach your goals, do you fear life without the support of another? This is the time to possibly see an individual therapist to help you separate and gain your own strength.

Boundary Structures

Now that we know what is important to us and what we don't want. And we know how to balance that in a relationship. It is important to review the other dynamics that exists around the topic of boundaries.

Knowing our boundaries and setting them are two very different hurdles to overcome. Setting boundaries does not always come easily. It's often a skill that needs to be learned and practiced. As renowned psychologist Albert Bandura noted, much of human social learning comes from modeling behavior, so if we do not have adequate role models whose behavior we can encode through observation and later imitate, we are at a loss, often left fumbling and frustrated.

Boundaries can be defined as the **limits we set** with other people

These limits indicate what we find **acceptable** and **unacceptable** in their behavior towards us. Additionally, boundaries can be defined as the limits and expectations we set for ourselves.

The ability to know and understand your boundaries generally comes from a healthy sense of self-worth or the ability to value yourself in a way that is not contingent on other people or the feelings they have toward you. *Self-worth means finding intrinsic value in who you are, so that you can be aware of the following*:

> ➤ Your intellectual worth and boundaries (you are entitled to your own thoughts and opinions, as are others.)
> ➤ Your emotional worth and boundaries (you are entitled to your own feelings in a given situation, as are others.)
> ➤ Your physical worth and boundaries (you are entitled to your space, however wide it may be, as are others.)
> ➤ Your social worth and boundaries (you are entitled to your own friends and to the pursuit of your own social activities, as are others.)
> ➤ Your spiritual worth and boundaries (you are entitled to your own spiritual beliefs, as are others.)

Different Types of Boundaries:

Rigid boundaries: this person avoids intimacy and close relationships, is unlikely to ask for help, has few close friendships, is very protective of personal information, may seem detached even with romantic partners and keeps others at a distance to avoid the possibility of rejection.

Porous boundaries: this person overshares personal information, has difficulty saying no to others, is over-involved with the problems of others, is dependent on the opinion of others, accepts abuse or disrespect and fears rejection if they do not comply with others.

Healthy boundaries: this person values their own opinions, doesn't compromise their values for others, shares personal information in an appropriate way, knows personal wants and needs and can communicate them but is accepting when others say 'no' to them.

It's time to go practice. Pay attention to your interactions, your boundaries, and your belief about your needs.

Chapter Five – Developing Self-Worth

The ability to know and understand your boundaries generally comes from a healthy sense of self-worth or the ability to value yourself in a way that is not contingent on other people or the feelings they have toward you. "citation"

Self-worth means finding fundamental value in who you are, so that you can be aware of the following:

➢ Your intellectual worth and boundaries (you are entitled to your own thoughts and opinions, as are others.)
➢ Your emotional worth and boundaries (you are entitled to your own feelings in a given situation, as are others.)
➢ Your physical worth and boundaries (you are entitled to your space, however wide it may be, as are others.)
➢ Your social worth and boundaries (you are entitled to your own friends and to the pursuit of your own social activities, as are others.)
➢ Your professional worth (you are entitled in your goal of earning money, to develop your professional/work path in a way that suits your goals and personality, as are others.)
➢ Your spiritual worth and boundaries (you are entitled to your own spiritual beliefs, as are others.)

What does this all mean? It means letting go of the fear of what others think. In this day (21st Century), as advanced as we are as people, we are more fearful of not being accepted, liked, approved of, and validated by others. Why has this happened over the decades. Many researchers have different opinions, but one common theory is the unintended result of social media. Everyone is connected to everyone else, and we watch each other's lives daily. We watch to see what others have, what they like, what they achieved, all their "really good stuff", and we want to have it, to fit in. We don't want to be too different. Different is bad and people don't accept different.

Over time, all these fears have made many people weaker regarding their own **self-worth**. Now I'm not trying to say that diversity is bad, in fact, it is what makes us better as society. However, one consequence is that many people struggle to know what is the "right" way to be. (Haug, J; American Thinker, 2013)

And not knowing the "right" way to be, or not being the "right way" depending on what group you are in, or want to be in, can make us feel; wrong.

Now I'm not suggesting we stop being diverse. People need to be aware of what is driving some of the confusion. In the reality, what I believe based on so many conversations with so many different people, is that people as a collective, our "society" really wants to have a "live and let live" aspect. Unfortunately, we just don't know how to get there. And as any therapist or psychologist would say, we can't control others, we can only control our reaction to others.

What does this mean for **self-worth** then? Well, it means that you should aim to "live" (and let live). Don't worry about what others think, believe, or want. Let everyone liveim their lives, let people find *fundamental values in themselves*. And you do the same. Be reciprocal, be respectful, and set boundaries (not just for them, but for yourself).

Self-Worth Components

Understand the power of your own attitude towards yourself.

- ➢ How you perceive yourself, how you talk to yourself about yourself, and how you represent yourself eventually becomes the reality for you.
- ➢ Start today, acknowledge your skills and weaknesses. Don't over-inflate your talents, don't belittle what you are not good at. Be honest and be okay with who you are.

Learn to embrace the power of self-love.

- ➢ In simplistic terms, treat yourself like you would treat others. If you would help your friend, then help yourself, if you would tell them something nice, tell yourself. Your family and friends shouldn't get more goodness than you give yourself.
- ➢ Start today changing the way you give to yourself.

Trust your feelings

- ➢ Self-worth means you need to honor your feelings. Learn to trust the way you feel about people, situations, and events. And don't automatically adjust or accept the feelings of others. When you trust your feelings, you can identify unfair demands on yourself.
- ➢ Start today, honor your feelings first.

Grow your ability to be self-aware and self-reflect.

- ➢ In modern times, we've been taught to seek the approval of others. To build your self-worth, you need to focus more on self-acceptance, self-reflection, and self-growth.
- ➢ Starting today, remind yourself about your talents, experiences, and skills.

Stop making your self-worth conditional on the opinions of

other people.

- ➤ When trying to live up to the expectations of others, whether parents, friends, spouses, or the media, people tend to find themselves struggling with a sense of personal identity and self-worth.
- ➤ Starting today, take ownership of the decisions for your life. Recognize that people can't know you better than you know yourself, even parents.
- ➤ Starting today, be okay if someone chooses to let you go from their life because you won't do what they "suggest". In this case, what they are saying is, "if you don't live life by my rules, then you can't be in my life." Don't become a prisoner to people. You will meet other people, create a new family.

Recognize that your inner voice, your perception of yourself, and how to represent yourself can become your reality.

- ➤ Your attitude about yourself has more power than people realize. When you minimize yourself, when you put the talents or skills of others above your own, and when you make yourself last, you have the power to create a life that does not benefit you.

➤ Starting today no more minimizing. For example, no more saying, "well, they are better than me anyway," "well, I didn't deserve to win anyway," "well, they are smarter than me," and the list could go on. Honor yourself by accepting your talents and skills. Say thank you if you get a compliment, don't explain away the compliment.

➤ Starting today look in the mirror and start accepting and liking the person who looks back. It might take some time and it may even feel uncomfortable, but it's worth it. You are worth it.

➤ Learn to support self-love. Some believe that self-love is a form of narcissism, selfishness, or arrogance (I've said that before, see how much it comes up). That would be wrong. Self-love is about supporting oneself and encouraging others to do the same. Healthy self-love is about being your own best friend. So, before you do something for someone else, do for yourself first.

Self-Care Highlight

51/49 Rule:

51 % of your spare energy (outside of work and sleep) goes to YOU. Then 49% goes to everyone else, that includes spouse/partner, kids, parents, friends, volunteer, etc.

Self-Worth Exercise:

Learn to trust your own feelings. Now, this can be different than letting your emotions make all the decisions. When you learn to understand and trust your feelings, it means you can name the feeling word that matches what you are going through. It's being able to say, "I'm scared I will fail this test because I didn't study." "I'm a bit excited to try this new thing." "I'm a little lonely tonight because my best friend moved away."

When you can acknowledge the true feeling in the moment, then you can honor what you need.

☆ Starting today, don't let anyone tell you, "You should be upset by that...," "you should be so angry at them, "don't worry about that, it shouldn't make you upset," "you are just a worrier, it doesn't really matter." Know how you feel and acknowledge it, don't let anyone tell you your feelings are wrong or invalid. Just make sure they are based on a solid situation, a fact, and not an imaged circumstance (review the cognitive distortions).

Finally, learn how to self-analyze. This means being able to self-critique, without being self-critical. Too many times in this day, we look to others to tell us about ourselves, as mentioned before, no one knows us better than we know ourselves.

☆ Starting today, learn how to self-reflect. For example, as yourself, "did I complete the tasks I wanted to, if within reason and if I didn't, why." It is okay to ask yourself why you didn't do something. If there is a legitimate reason, then give grace, but if you watched television too long, then be accountable to yourself. This isn't about self-condemning or self-criticizing; it is learning to be accountable. We cannot grow in our values and in our character, if we can't hold ourselves to the same standards, we want others to rise to.

Start practicing growing your self-worth today.

Finish the sentences below (all positive viewpoints):

I create:

_____

_____

I deserve:

_____

_____

I can:

_____

_____

I will:

_____

_____

I trust:

_____

I love:

_____

I have:

_____

I feel:

_____

I believe:

_____

_____

I AM:

_____

_____

_____

_____

I AM (practice again):

_____

_____

_____

_____

I AM (practice again):

_____

_____

_____

_____

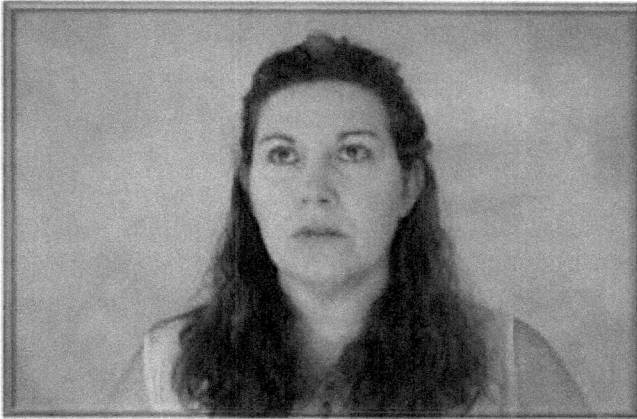

Chapter Six - Building Self-Confidence

Self-confidence is the ability to trust in your own judgment and abilities. It is about accepting yourself completely despite our imperfections. In fact, self-confidence is stronger when you can acknowledge both your talents and flaws.

Self-efficacy (positive belief about your own capabilities) and **self-esteem** (confidence in one's own worth or abilities) are sometimes used interchangeably with **self-confidence**. No matter which words we select it is all about *having a positive belief in oneself*.

For example, I like to bake. I like the precision of it. But I cannot cook well. For me baking a dessert is not the same as cooking a steak on the grill. I assume people who grill as thinking to themselves, "heck yeah."

Self-confidence can exist when I say, "I am good at baking, and not good at cooking." I acknowledge my skills at baking, without feeling selfish (I am not minimizing any other person or their skills, just acknowledging my own). AND I am confident that I am not a good cook. The fact is, I can't smell the difference between herbs. I don't taste the difference either. I don't like to guess as quantity. These are legitimate reasons why I struggle, and because I struggle, I don't practice, which is why I am not good at it. This doesn't mean I can't cook anything. I do have a few meals I can cook. But I'll never have the same skills as baking.

I hope you can see how I acknowledge what I am good at, and also acknowledge what I am not good at. I am not self-critical, self-depreciating, or self-minimizing.

It is what it is.

That is self-confidence. I am happy with my talents, and I am happy with my failings (in the kitchen).

How do you build self-confidence? You must try things. And then when you try something, you self-analyze. You talk to yourself about the experience, what you learned, what you already knew. Self-confidence comes from life experiences; it comes from knowing yourself.

How do we build our sense of self? The first thing we need to do is get to know ourselves. Let's do an exercise.

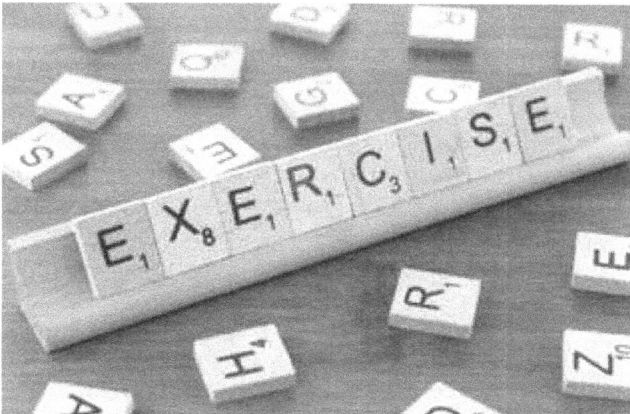

Self-Confidence Exercise:

Who Are You?

Let's answer a few questions to get a
sense of who you are:

Which season are you:
Winter , Spring, Summer
Fall _____

Which do you prefer:
Pants, shorts, or dresses:

_____

Which do you prefer:
Tennis, sandals, formal
shoes, or slippers:

_____

Which do you prefer:
Mornings, Afternoons or
Evenings:

_____

Which do you prefer:
Beach or Mountains?

_____

Which do you prefer:
Rain or Sunshine?

_____

Which do you prefer:
Hot or cold weather?

_____

Which do you prefer:
City, Suburbs, or Rural?

_____

Which color are you:
Blue(s), Red(s), Green(s),
Orange(s), Purple(s),
Yellow(s)?

_____

What type of food do you
prefer? (Mexican, Asian,
American, Greek,
Mediterranean, etc?

_____

What type of music do
you prefer?(Country,
Rock, Pop, R&B, Rap, etc)

_____

Are you a night owl or
early bird?

_____

What is your favorite
accessory?

_____

What is your favorite
movie genre??

_____

What is your favorite
vacation spot??

_____

Are you introvert,
extrovert, or combo??

Now that you went through the list and answered the questions, take a moment to pause and keep going. Write the words all over the page if you need. Include any "buzz" words that you feel describe you.

_____

_____

_____

_____

_____

_____

_____

_____

_____

~ pause ~

How does it feel to see YOU on that page? It is these things that you listed that make you who you are. And knowing who you are came from the experiences in your life. I bet if you look back at each word, you know why you picked that word.

For example, I prefer summer to winter, and spring to fall, but summer first, then fall, then spring and then winter.

How do I know the seasons that specifically? Because I have lived in different states, gone through the four seasons many times, and found which ones make me smile (warmth of summer), which ones make me grimace (winter cold). Which ones help me enjoy growth (spring flowers blooming) and which ones help me enjoy change (fall and the leaves changing colors).

It is the experiences that helped me know me, which gave me confidence in who I am.

Don't let anyone tell you that you are wrong about YOU. Be who you are and enjoy it. Love being unique.

And if you found there were questions or areas that you couldn't answer, then go have an experience. And preferably do it alone the first time, that way you are not clouded by the opinion of another person.

Here are some suggestions:

- ➢ Go to a zoo
- ➢ Go to an aquarium
- ➢ Go to a botanical garden
- ➢ Go to a new restaurant
- ➢ Try a new dish at an old restaurant
- ➢ Try a different color shirt (get out of your standard colors)
- ➢ Find a free class (there is a website that offers discounts)
- ➢ Find a small town and go to one of their events
- ➢ Go to a new festival
- ➢ Bake or cook a dish you've never tried before
- ➢ Visit another State, if you can, take a road trip
- ➢ Finger paint
- ➢ Sing out loud in your back yard
- ➢ Put together a puzzle
- ➢ Plant some seeds (flowers or veggies)
- ➢ Read a novel
- ➢ Volunteer for a day

Chapter Seven - Lose the BUT, Embrace the "AND"

One of the most difficult aspects to feeling secure and confidence is balancing perspective. Perspective shapes how reality can influence our thoughts, beliefs, and worldview. So why does perspective cause us so many problems. Simply, everyone has a different worldview, and therefore a different take on the same situations.

For example, if I put two people on a roller coaster ride, they can have the exact same experience, but perspective (aka worldview, beliefs) can cause those two people to feel very differently about the ride. One may love the turns, but the other gets nauseated. One may love the speed, but the other is fearful. One may love the loops, but the other doesn't like the head rush.

One experience two different

perspectives. Which one is correct? The fact is, they both are. They both are for each person. The goal is to acknowledge all perspectives/worldviews as valid without dismissing our own views.

In other words, how I feel about this is right for me. It is this reason that so many people don't understand how they disagree. Most people don't believe we (other people) will agree on everything, but knowing that, they still don't understand how someone could think differently. Again, this is why confidence is so important, so we can effectively express how we feel about something (no matter if its negative or positive) and then we can sit with that and hold it, even if someone doesn't understand it.

What happens when we have our own different perspective about a situation?

For example, you go to a play that you are iffy about. You might think "that was a good play, BUT it was really expensive." And then internally you might struggle because "it was a good play," BUT "now I am broke." That internal battle happens because you are more focused on the fact that you are now broke. The "but" stops us thinking about the first half of that sentence. We might only focus on the "but," "but it was really expensive." When we talk to people about the play, we say a few words, but internally we are not happy because it was expensive.

➢ First thing that comes to mind is, boundaries. Why did you pay for a ticket if it was going to leave you broke? If you do this, go back, and review the Setting Boundaries chapters.

➢ Second thing is, if you were okay with being broke, you really wanted to see the play, then stop saying but. But can effectively negate the first half of the sentence.

"And" Exercises:

See the difference between the two sentences:

1. The play was good, but it was expensive.
2. The play was good, and it was expensive.

1. He yelled at me last night, but he is normally a good listener.
2. He yelled at me last night and he is normally a good listener.

1. She is late again, but she is very busy.
2. She is late again, and she is very busy.

When you read them, can you hear the difference in the sentences. With the "but," the sentence can feel more negative, and we stop focusing on the first half. With the "and" we are considering both sides of the comment.

This is more effective when looking at our perspective and others' perspectives. Ask yourself, am I negating the first half, or is the other person negating the first half. Is our perspective skewed.

1. I'm sorry your father passed away, but he is not in pain anymore.
2. I'm sorry your father passed away and he is not in pain anymore.

1. I know break ups hurt, but there is someone else.
2. I know break ups hurt and there is someone else.

In these two cases, they are difficult situations, where the speaker could have had a better "second half of the sentence", maybe one that was more compassionate. When you read them, you can see that the "and" still makes it better. Granted not necessarily comments I would make, but the **but** makes it worse.

Starting today, try to use the AND and see what happens.

Examples:

I'm tired and I'll do my best at work.

I'm sad over a loss and I'll keep going.

I'm scared I'll get fired and I'm still going to give it my best shot.

Embrace that both perspectives can be true and are both legitimate and both need to be acknowledged. Humans are complex and we are dynamic. It doesn't benefit us to focus on only one aspect of our feelings, emotions, beliefs in a given situation.

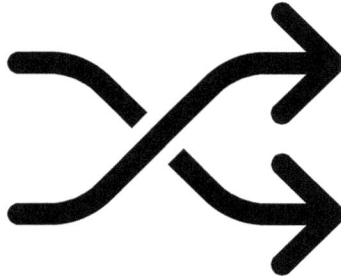

Now you try:

_____

_____

_____

_____

_____

_____

_____

_____

_____

_____

_____

_____

_____

_____

_____

_____

_____

Chapter Eight - Active Mindfulness

You may or may not have heard about mindfulness or grounding. Mindfulness is the more common term of the two. People may also use meditation, which includes mindfulness.

Let me explain why mindfulness, meditation, and/or grounding can be beneficial for anxious thinking and the physiological response that comes with it.

With "anxiety", when you think of the past, present, or future, where do you think your thoughts spend most of their time. My experience would suggest that you are spending a large amount of your mental energy focusing on past events or future events, but not so much energy on the here and now.

The pit fall of this type of cognition is that we are missing the here and now. If you do go out to socialize with a friend, they might even say to you, "you are here, but not here." And then you may even feel bad, guilty, or sad that you couldn't enjoy yourself. And now this moment, which was supposed to be fun or at least enjoyable, has now become another moment in your past that you are worrying about, and wonder if in the future, they will want to meet again, if they still want to be your friend, and possibly even what do they now think of me.

Anxiety doesn't allow us to enjoy today.

I want to remind everyone, that this book is primarily focused on generalized anxiety or social, but not necessarily trauma-based anxiety. With a trauma-based anxiety, you might feel distress, worry or anxiousness <u>right now</u> because of being in an abusive or toxic situation. That is a real issue because your fear may be very valid, the fear of getting hurt emotionally or physically, right now, and right now what do I do. If this is the case, seek support from a coach, pastor, or therapist.

A little side note, some people may see their current "anxiety" as trauma based from a time prior in their life. Then you still might benefit from this book as you are not in present and real fear, danger, or abuse. Also, I'm not going to review the definition of trauma. Trauma can be different for everyone based on situation, age at time, length of exposure, etc. Please use your best judgment or seek guidance from a therapist.

I don't want to skip over meditation, which is also a process of calming, focusing, and relaxing. There are many types of meditation, but most have four fundamentals in common: a quiet location with as few distractions as possible; a specific, comfortable posture (sitting, lying down, walking, or in other positions); a focus of attention (a specially chosen word or set of words, an object, or the sensations of the breath); and an open attitude (letting distractions come and go naturally without judging them).

Mindfulness

Mindfulness is the intentional act of fully paying attention to what is happening around you, to what you're doing, to the space you're moving through right now in this moment. That might seem inconsequential, except for the annoying fact that we so often veer from the present. Our mind starts to drift, we lose touch with our body, and soon we're engrossed in obsessive thoughts about something that just happened or fretting about the future. And that makes us anxious.

Incredibly though, mindfulness is the technique that can bring us back to where we are and what we're doing and feeling. And like the other chapters in this book, I'm hoping you will practice, so that you can experience what I'm suggesting rather than just reading about it.

Because mindfulness is rising in popularity you will find resources through websites, blogs, videos, and books. Feel free to do more research, **knowledge is power.**

Again, the basic definition of mindfulness is:

the ability to be fully present, aware of where you are and what you're doing, and not be overly reactive or unreactive by what's going on around you.

Mindfulness is not something that we are necessarily taught to engage in, but it is a skill that all humans have, to varying degrees. Like many things, it can be developed through different techniques and many people have many different styles. Mindfulness can be done by laying, sitting, walking, and slow moving.

For someone learning this technique, one rule of thumb is, go into it without judgement (how good will I be) or goal setting (I need to achieve this much). These different dynamics can change the tone of the practice itself. You may put too much pressure on yourself to succeed. And aren't we already anxious enough?

The result we are looking for, through mindfulness, is to gain time back in our lives. Not time on a clock, but emotional time, cognitive time. To gain experiences and connection that we may be missing by being focused on the past or the future.

Mindful Exercise:

1. **Get comfortable:** Sit, stay, walk, lay down if you won't fall asleep. Just get comfortable. **I prefer to walk because time outdoors is good for the body and soul.**
2. **Decide how much time you will practice.** In the beginning 5 – 10 minutes is enough.
3. **Start to focus on the things around you** (sidewalk, trees, chair, lamp, etc.). This is grounding, you can get more details about grounding on the next page.
4. **If your mind wanders, let it.** Don't judge yourself for it, the best practice occurs because our mind wanders. The practice is to just come back to the present.

5. **Mindfulness is not meant to be complicated:** Moments of mindfulness should happen through things that are familiar to us because it's what we already do, how we already are. Don't change you, just change how you are in the moment.
6. **Mindfulness is not meant to be an "add on":** People naturally can be present. However, we may need to practice and cultivate these innate skills.
7. **The goal is to make it a way of living:** For mindfulness to be most effective, *it requires practice*. Making it a part of our daily lives helps bring awareness and caring into everything we do—and it cuts down needless stress. Even a little less stress can make our lives better.
8. **It's evidence-based:** We don't have to take mindfulness on faith. Both science and experience demonstrate its positive benefits for our health, happiness, work, and relationships.

Grounding

Grounding is a type of coping strategy that is designed to "ground" you in, or connect you with, the present moment. Grounding is often used for flashbacks or dissociation that might be associated with post-traumatic stress disorder (PTSD). Because of its focus on being present in the moment, grounding is a part of mindfulness. It can also be a method of distraction to get you out of your head and away from upsetting thoughts, memories, or feelings.

How Grounding Works

➢ Grounding techniques use the five senses—sound, touch, smell, taste, and sight—to connect you with the here and now. For example, singing a song, rubbing lotion on your hands, or sucking on some sour candies are all grounding techniques that produce sensations that are difficult to ignore or distract you from what's going on in your mind. This helps you directly and instantaneously connect with the present moment.

➢ Grounding is highly personal. What may work for one person may trigger discomfort in another. You may need to do research on yourself before you figure out which grounding techniques work best for you. Pay attention to the coping techniques you've already developed to see if you can convert any of the into a grounding moment.

➢ Grounding doesn't have to be complex. Grounding can be as simple as taking off one's shoes, and walking barefoot in the ground, which has been proven beneficial for anxiousness and nerves. Grounding is a good way to connect with oneself and the earth to bring yourself back into the moment.

Grounding Techniques

To connect with the here and now, do something (or several things) that will bring all your attention to the present moment. Be sure to keep your eyes open while you're grounding yourself so you're aware of everything that's going on around you. With the grounding techniques you are looking to find ways to awaken, focus, or shock our senses which stops our brain from focusing on the anxious feeling.

Here are practice suggestions:

Sound

- Crank up the radio and blast your favorite song.
- Talk out loud about what you see, hear, or what you're thinking or doing.
- Call a loved one.
- Put on some nature sounds such as birds chirping or waves crashing.
- Read out loud, whether it's a favorite children's book, a blog article, or the latest novel.

Touch

- Hold an ice cube and let it melt in your hand.
- Put your hands under running water.
- Take a hot or cool shower.
- Hold onto a soft sweater, pillow, or blanket.
- Rub your hand lightly over the carpet or a piece of furniture, noting the texture.
- Pop some bubble wrap.
- Massage your temples.
- If you have a dog or cat, cuddle and pet him or her.
- Drink a hot or cold beverage.

Smell

- Sniff strong peppermint, which also has the benefit of having a soothing effect.
- Light a scented candle or melt scented wax.

- Get some essential oils (freshly cut grass, rain, clean laundry, or sugar cookies, for example) and smell one.
- Even smelling pepper from your kitchen will work.

Taste

- Bite into a lemon or lime.
- Suck on a mint or chew peppermint or cinnamon gum.
- Take a bite of a pepper or some hot salsa, hot candies as well.
- Let a piece of chocolate melt in your mouth, noticing how it tastes and feels as you roll it around with your tongue.

Sight

- Make a mental list of everything around you.
- Count all the pieces of furniture around you.
- Put on your favorite movie or TV show.
- Play a distracting game on your tablet, computer, or smartphone.
- Complete a crossword puzzle, sudoku, word search, or other puzzles.
- Read a book or magazine.

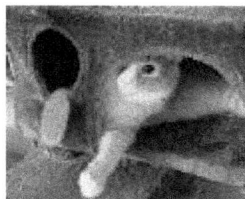

Grounding Can Be Done Anywhere!!

I believe the best part about grounding is it can be done anywhere. My favorite thing to do is walk and observe life around me.

If I am indoors, I might find a hallway and pay attention to the silence, to look at the carpet colors or design, to feel the air conditioning or heating flow through the area.

If I am outside, which is my most favorite, to walk and really take in deep breaths to feel the fresh air. I listen to the wind through the trees, to the birds and even to the cars around me. I listen for the dogs barking and strange sounds I can't identify. I feel the breeze across my face and if it is warm, I'll notice the sweat run down the side of my face. And when I am really prepared, I will even bring a little snack with me and chew little bites as I walk. For those 5 or 10 minutes that I am walking, there is nothing else in the world except that moment.

Grounding Exercise:

Working on grounding can take practice because we might start with judging how fast am I walking, or did I listen correctly, etc. With practice, mindfulness becomes easier over time. Remember though, if these suggestions don't work, try something different. Each person is different and what helps us feel connected is very different. For my grandmother, it was baking. The woman rarely ate her own desserts, but she would spend so much time baking. She really enjoyed the experience of mixing, blending, pouring, baking in the oven, a little taste. Her calm space was in the kitchen. Which wasn't bad until she moved into a great retirement community. My only concern was her feeding everyone too much sugar. But they never seemed to complain. Ultimately her grounding place and activity was also a win for her neighbors.

Start to practice. See what works for you. And if you think to yourself, "why am I practicing"? Then answer yourself with "if I am practicing now, and making it a lifestyle now, then for just a few moments each day, I am not worrying. And image if you were to practice mindfulness or grounding twice a day, just for 10 minutes. Image where your skills can go from there and how much calmer you might feel.

Chapter Nine - Positive Coping Skills

One of the first questions I ask most new clients is, "what do you do for fun." You may or may not believe this but about 90% of the time, I get a blank stare back. That question can stop a conversation. Which is okay, because then it introduces a good topic: positive coping skills, having fun, and self-care.

Self-care is a part of positive coping skills and is a big aspect to reducing anxiety. This might seem like a natural concept, however, many people that have high anxiety don't engage in regular self-care activities.

In fact, for the research I did for my dissertation, I found out that 86% of American's don't engage in regular physical activity. If we aren't moving and having fun, then what are we doing most of the time? This might answer questions about why we do have so much "anxiety" now.

Part of the reason that people give me for not engaging in self-care is they are:

➢ too tired
➢ too broke
➢ too alone
➢ too busy
➢ too "something"

But if you never take care of yourself, how do you keep going?

It is like putting yourself on a hamster wheel and then wondering why your anxiousness, stress, or tiredness just won't go away.

Some people have suggested to me in the past, that taking a shower or a walk, isn't going to reduce their worry. And the reality is, that may be correct. A shower can't make a bill go away, it can't make a shy person feel good in a crowd, it can't make us do anything. But what it can do is give us a moment to pause, to rest our brains, and to downshift so that we have the mental energy to do those things. Image if you just sat and listened to water run, to just feel the warmth of the water on your skin, to just be still in that moment. The goal is that it is relaxing, calming. And then in the next moment, you may have the emotional energy to manage the worry. That is what positive coping skills and self-care are for.

As we discussed earlier, anxiety is about the past or the future, and not about right now. There are exceptions, for example social anxiety, but even that, is worrying about what will others think (which is a future thought, even though it may be an immediate future). With anxiety, we will split hairs and get technical from time to time.

Anyway, Self-care is about taking care of ourselves so that we can manage the stuff in our life. And it is a very important part of our lives. Think about it, don't you get the oil changed in your car, don't you throw away expired food, don't you wash your clothes? Of course, you are doing all these things to "take care of a car, stomach, and clothing". So then why not take care of you, the person.

Let's talk about what self-care is.

Self-care is doing things that promote your mind, body, or soul. Yes, that hot shower is to clean your body, so you don't smell. But it is also to help you relax, quiet your mind, hide from young children, and have 10 minutes of silence. Self-care typically has many sides to it. The question is, are Positive Coping skills different? Yes, they are the skills or tools specifically to feel good. That shower is a positive coping skill, as well as just being a shower. Distraction is one form of positive coping skill.

144

Distraction and Grounding

I think most of us know what distraction is, but if not, the result is to redirect your own cognition (thinking) from one thing to another. Distraction can last from 15 minutes to a couple hours. Within distraction is also "grounded" distraction. Grounding is a form of mindfulness. We reviewed that in the previous chapter. As a reminder, grounding focuses on our five senses (seeing, smelling, tasting, touching, and hearing).

Distraction and Grounding Exercise:

Let's start thinking of a list of things we can do. Don't worry about how long it takes, let's come up with a list.

_____

_____

_____

_____

_____

_____

_____

_____

_____

_____

Self-care Specifics

Self-care is doing anything that helps you feel good. It could be laying on the couch for a bit watching television, it could be doing a few things around the house to feel like you have accomplished something. But it also could be going to get a sweet treat. It could be buying yourself a new pair of shoes or getting a fresh haircut. Self-care should make you feel good.

Self-Care Exercise:

Let's start thinking of a list of things we can do. Don't worry about how long it takes, let's come up with a list.

_____

_____

_____

_____

_____

_____

_____

_____

_____

_____

Emotional Release

Another positive coping skill is **emotional release**. Sometimes we just need to feel those emotions. If you are sad, am I suggesting you cry. I am!! Cry so you can release that energy. If you can't seem to bring it up, then I always recommend watching a movie with a dog in it. Has there ever been a movie where the dog is not lost, hurt, scared, etc. Dog movies always make me cry.

Are you ready to be done crying? Are you ready to laugh, but just can't get there? Pull up YouTube and watch a funny video. Find your favorite comedian, get a good laugh that way. Now, are you angry, maybe you need to yell and scream. No, not at someone, how about alone in your car. Yes, everyone does laugh at me when I recommend that. But you know, sometimes a good scream helps.

The end goal is 1), feel those feelings, and 2), release that energy.

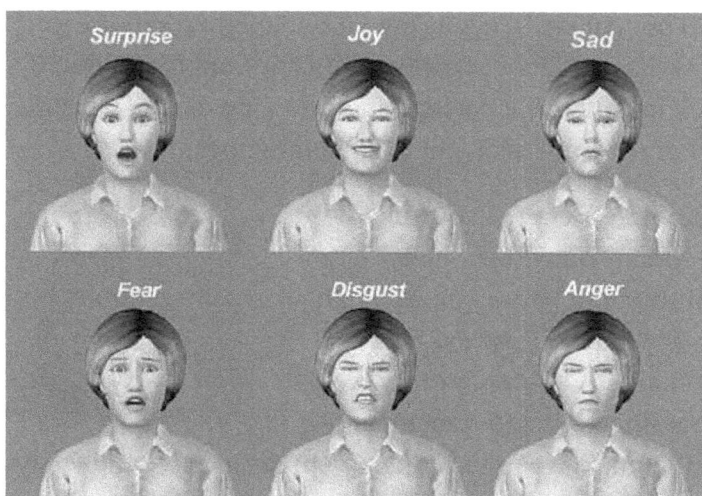

Emotional Release Exercise:

What emotions do you need to work on releasing and what might be a good way for you to release them?

_____

_____

_____

_____

_____

_____

_____

Thought Challenge

Thought challenge is one of the toughest AND most useful coping skills. It is about challenging your thinking, to see if you are stuck in a negative perception. If you are, can you change the concept of the self-statement to something positive.

For example, if you tell yourself, "I always forget something on my to do list, I'm so dumb." Can you turn that around to, "Maybe I put too many things on my to-do list for one day, making it impossible to remember everything, maybe I can spread my chores over a couple days."

Can you also "check-in" with yourself just to ensure there are no **cognitive distortions** happening. For example, "what is the evidence to prove this is true," "what would a friend say about my thoughts," "would I tell a friend what I am telling myself."

Thought challenge can help us redirect our thinking so that it is healthy and balanced. I won't say that it must be all positive, accountability is okay, but belittling yourself is not.

Thought Challenge Exercise:

Write a sentence down, and if it has negative undertones, then rewrite it with a positive slant. Get help with this one if you need.

_____

_____

_____

_____

_____

_____

_____

_____

_____

Helping Others

And then my favorite, looking to help someone else. I get mixed responses on this, but the reason we look to doing something for someone else, is it makes us feel good and we are not thinking about our worry for a little bit, we are thinking about them. There is something very powerful in stepping outside your own worry for a little bit to help another person.

Now, I'm not saying that you must make it a big gesture. It can be something simple. Holding the door open for another person is a very gracious thing. Maybe the next time you are at a grocery store and someone there is in a wheelchair, and they are trying to get something off a high shelf. Maybe lend them a hand. If you want to do more, you can.

Many organizations need volunteers. Volunteering is something I really enjoy doing. I've rarely gone to an organization where they really need help, and they are mean. They are normally so happy to have help, they are gracious. I find it easy to talk to people because we have a "built in" topic. We are doing something, so I don't feel too awkward. And you can give as however much of your time you have to spare. Again, they just appreciate anything.

Helping Others Exercise:

Let's start thinking of a list of ways we can help. Don't worry about how long it takes, let's come up with a list.

I'll get you started:

> Local non-profit
> Girl Scouts or Boy Scouts
> Big Brother or Big Sisters
> Food Pantry / Food Bank
> United Way

_____

_____

_____

_____

_____

_____

Negative coping skills

Let's shift gears for a moment, I keep talking about Positive Coping skills. Are there negative coping skills, yes. Definitely!!

In fact, several people report feeling worse and get stuck on that hamster wheel because they are using negative coping skills.

If I go out to lunch with my friends, food and socializing are a great coping skill. But if I sit at home and eat a full pizza, ice cream, and drink a few sodas, then food and isolation have become a negative coping skill. Please don't think I am trying to make fun of anyone, but this is a reality for some people. The reality is staying inside and being alone for too many days at a time is harmful for our mental health. And eating too many unhealthy carbs and sugars is harmful for our physical health. And the difficult part is, we don't always see the negative cycle begin.

You might think, today is just a bad day, so I'll get my favorite pizza. Okay, that is fine. But then the next day is bad too, and then it's okay for a couple days, and then its bad again and again and each time it is bad, I'm eating.

I am picking on food, but it can also be alcohol, caffeine, gambling, sex, shopping, work, going out, isolating, and the list can go on. This is also why I also recommend a variety of positive coping skills, to really reinforce that one negative one is not worth it. You will have multiple skills to replace it with.

Before we end this chapter, let's go back to the positive side.

The moment of "choice"

Think about that fork in the road, that moment you can pick a negative coping skill or a positive coping skill. How do you think you would feel if you were able to?

> ➤ make a healthier choice
> ➤ do something nice or fun
> ➤ have a distraction for a while that just took your mind off other things for a bit

Moment of Choice Exercise:

Just for today, make a different choice, one that is supportive of yourself, kind, and positive. And write it down.

Then tomorrow, repeat. Keep writing down what choice you made differently.

_____

_____

_____

_____

_____

_____

_____

_____

Chapter 10 - Exercise and Nutrition

At the time of writing this book, in addition to being a Health Psychologist, I am also a Certified Mental Health Integrative Medicine Provider. I am focusing on this integration because I believe in the combination of psychology, social, health (and wellness).

I am not speaking as a registered dietitian, an exercise physiologist, or a personal trainer. Those are specialties which dive deeper in those specific areas. Previously I've said in the book, if you need someone specific, such as a coach, pastor, or therapist to seek out the help you need. This time, I am adding the skills of physical therapists, registered dietitians, exercise physiologist, nutrition specialists, or others in this area.

Up to this point in the book, the chapters have covered a lot with the mind (cognitive distortions, feelings and emotions, worldview, boundaries, etc.). Now we are going to look at basic skills that help the body. As a disclaimer, do not make any large changes without the consultation of your primary care doctor, especially if you have any medical conditions.

"We are what we repeatedly do. Excellence then is not an act but a habit." ~ Aristotle

Healthy Eating

Healthy eating focuses on maintaining or improving overall health through nutrition choice. A healthy diet includes balanced nutrition: fluids, macronutrients, micronutrients, and adequate amounts of food to balance energy needs.

If you are unfamiliar with what you need, especially if you have specific health needs, consult a professional. Don't resist getting support. It is an act of self-care.

Now, one important statement:

All food is good food!!

I'm not going to tell you to quit specific foods. What I want you to do is to decide what is best for your health.

Grocery Shopping

A simple rule: 90% of your grocery purchases should come from the outside/boarder of the store.

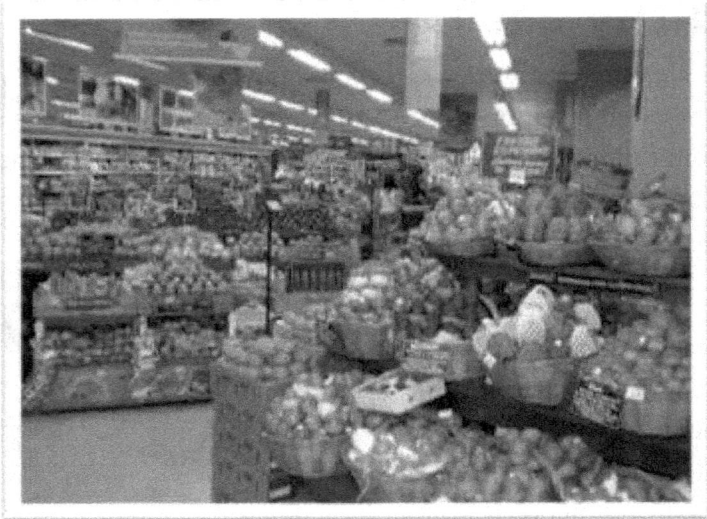

What I mean is, if you enter a grocery store and you scan around, you will typically see fruits and veggies, dairy, and meats. You will also catch other type items that may or may not work for you such as bread and desserts. it's all about balanced nutrition and needs.

As you enter the grocery aisles, you will see more processed food: cereals, pastas, flavorings, frozen dinner, more desserts, etc. Again, I'm not saying all of this is bad, but processed food can carry with it unnecessary carbs, fats, sugars, etc. Again, "all food is good food," but we need balance. We need the items that come from the outside of the store more.

If you need some guidance, "choose my plate" is a great website. No website is ever perfect, but it can help you. It has tips, recommendations, and more. Again, **choosemyplate.gov**.

Portion Distortion

We just talked about getting our food, but we need to add in a sub-section to that, portion distortion. Recent research shows that portion sizes at dine-in and fast-food restaurants have increased in size. While the restaurant industry is trying to help consumers get the most out of their money, they are giving us more, and we are also eating more (United States Department of Agriculture, n.d.). The question is:

Do We Really Need More?

Food intake should be a balance to energy output. If you've had a chill day, binge watched television, and I agree that is great to do from time to time, if you go to a restaurant or fast food, do you really need supersize?

Growing **portion** sizes are changing what Americans think of as a "normal" **portion** at home too.

Pay attention to your energy output, it will be different depending on your work condition. For example, a construction worker may need more calories, nutrients, and food than a college student. A nurse who is running around all day may need more than an officer worker sitting at a desk.

When you go home to cook dinner, each plate should not look the same between you, your significant other/spouse, children, elder parents, etc. Each of you had a different kind of day.

At choosemyplate.gov/tools-portion-distortion see what the standard portion size was 20 years ago. Also learn which exercises are beneficial, especially if we want to burn off those favorite foods.

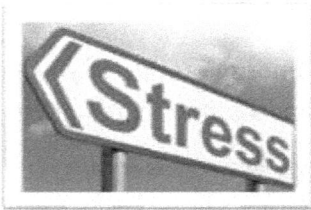

Food and Stress

My favorite topic is stress. It's such an "every person, every day" aspect to our lives. And stress is something that can genuinely affect our everyday health and wellness. Let's learn a little bit more about stress and food.

➤ Are you reaching for that comfort food during stressful times? If yes, that comfort food is reinforcing the bad habit that food reduces stress.

➤ Most likely those comfort foods are full of carbohydrates, when eaten, they release Serotonin, which makes us feel better. It can be a vicious cycle. And we don't tend to burn those unnecessary carb calories (some carbs benefit – everything in balance).

➤ The better option is to replace comfort food with other feel-good activity that promote overall better health (Annesi,

2013). One example is to drink teas that helps with calming.

➢ Stress eating tends to lead to overeating because we aren't mindful and present with our thoughts about the food. We just go through the mechanics of eating until we feel better. When we stress eat without mindful though, the random food that we don't need can fluctuate blood glucose levels making us feel tired, irritable, and disconnected.

A good lesson, get those 3 (to 6) meals a day, depending on how you balance your nutritional needs. To clarify, when I say 6 meals, 3 of those are standard breakfast, lunch, and dinner, the other 3 are small nutritious snacks that provide energy so that we don't get over hungry. For some, this doesn't work. Make sure you are eating in a way that works for you. That being said, one meal a day is not beneficial and can cause drops in blood sugar causing us to believe we are anxious, nervous, or on edge, when really our body is just needing nutrients.

Exercise and Physical Activity

Now, let's talk about the body from a physicality standpoint. What I mean is, are you moving your body. Did you know the World Health Organization recommends:

➢ Getting at least 30 minutes of exercise, 3 times a week, because it can help to reduce stress and promote weight balance.

➢ Exercise can be anything that raises the heartrate to a slightly higher rate than normal.

> ➤ Research shows that interval exercise is the most effective to increase metabolism for at least 24 hours post workout. Intervals consists of brief periods of intense effort into the workout; for example, 2 minutes fast, 4 minutes slow, and repeat (United States Department of Agriculture, n.d.).

> ➤ The exercise can be walking, jogging, or running. It can be completed outside or inside on a machine. It could also be from swimming, cycling, or stairs.

> ➤ Intervals should leave you breathing hard. Although always talk to your physician first before starting any new routines.

It's important to remember that our bodies are machines, they are meant to be worked. And if we can move our bodies and have fun, then even better. Keep a body positive attitude for a better and brighter outlook.

What is the difference between Exercise and Physical Activity?

> ➤ Exercise is planned, structured, repetitive, and intention movement intended to improve physical health.
> ➤ Physical activity is movement that is carried out by the skeletal muscles that requires energy. Basically, any movement is physical activity.

If you don't like formal exercise, find the fun in moving your body another way. Your body won't care, it just wants to move.

Healthy Eating and Exercise to Improve Overall Health

> ➤ Research shows that even slight changes to eating and exercise habits can promote weight loss or effective maintenance, reduce high blood pressure, and improve blood glucose.

In addition to mental health, increasing nutritious food choices and increasing physical activity can reduce stress and anxiety symptoms, which can also have a positive impact on weight loss (Annesi, 2013).

Nutrition and Physical Activity Exercise:

Let's pay attention for one week, keep a food journal and a physical activity journal. Write down what you are eating and how much you are moving your body, stretching your muscles.

Date/Time   Food/Physical Activity   Comments

_____

_____

_____

_____

_____

_____

Date/Time	Food/Physical Activity	Comments

Date/Time	Food/Physical Activity	Comments

Date/Time	Food/Physical Activity	Comments

Date/Time   Food/Physical Activity   Comments

_____

_____

_____

_____

_____

_____

_____

_____

_____

_____

_____

_____

_____

_____

_____

_____

_____

_____

_____

Chapter Eleven - Sleep

Sleep is one of the most crucial aspects to health living and reducing anxious feelings. According to the Sleep Foundation (2021) one third of Americans are sleep deprived. Yes, one third!! That is a lot of us out there extremely tired. And what happens when we are tired, we are more emotional, we are short tempered because we are working so hard to function, and we are not cognitively as clear. The next time you are driving, look around at the cars and think about it… one third of the people around you are sleep deprived.

Now I'm not trying to get you anxious, ironically, I am trying to help you become aware of the problem in the United States. And why is this important, because there might be a time that you say to yourself, "but most people in society are okay being tired." The reality is, yes, we Americans love to push ourselves, that is built into our society, but it doesn't mean we are always right and being sleep deprived is one area where we get it wrong.

Did you know there are sleep disorders? I point this out because I don't want you to assume what you are struggling with is "anxiety", again, that is an easy answer.

Sleep Disorders

The most common sleep disorders are:
➢ Insomnia
➢ Sleep apnea
➢ Narcolepsy
➢ Snoring
➢ Melatonin disruptions
➢ General sleep deprivation
➢ Night terrors
➢ Circadian rhythm disorders

If you are not sleeping consistently or well (a good night sleep), start with a medical checkup. A therapist can also help with mindfulness, meditation, racing thoughts, general sleep hygiene skills, and more (Sleep Foundation, 2021).

Going forward in this chapter there is an assumption that you are without any significant medical issues that would impair your sleep and you just need added extra skills.

Sleep Hygiene

What is sleep hygiene? Really, it is just good sleep habits. Yes, there are very specific "good sleep" behaviors. *Let's review them.

➢ Be consistent with your bedtime/wake time.
➢ Make sure your bedroom has the optimal setup.
➢ Review of electronics in the bedroom
➢ Try to avoid large meals late in the evening, caffeine after 2pm, and alcohol in the late evening before bed.
➢ Be physically active during the day.
➢ No naps or if you take one, keep it short.

*You can get more information from the CDC website.

I want to go a little more in depth into each of those bullet points.

> Be consistent - This is not just for little kids. The more consistent your sleep and wake time, the more stable your circadian rhythm. The weekend is no exception, keep as close to schedule even on the weekends (CDC, 2016).

> Optimal set up - Let's talk a little extra about the "bedroom setup". Make sure the room is dark, however, remember we need light to enter to help transition us to waking. Most people sleep better with a room that is a little cooler, and make sure your bed and pillow are comfortable.

> Electronics – some people will say have nothing in your bedroom and that might be necessary for some. However, for people who experience racing thoughts or who are active "thinkers," some electronics can be helpful. I never recommend watching tv, however listening to something you've seen a thousand times, and it is kind of boring can be helpful, or listening to a podcast (same thing, something you've heard) and listening to a sound machine. Basically, the act of "listening" can help us not "think", allowing us to fall asleep.

> Avoid meals, caffeine, and alcohol – while some people might have a late evening snack like yogurt, granola bar, fruit, etc., the reality is, we don't want our stomachs working hard to digest. Now caffeine, if you didn't already know, it is a stimulant. Need I say more? A stimulant does not help us before bed. As far as alcohol, yes, some will say they fall asleep with it, however did you know that alcohol can disrupt REM sleep? Alcohol is also a depressant so we can feel emotionally down while drinking it and after.

> ➤ Be active – our bodies are machines, and they need to have movement. If your body can, be active at least 4 days a week with at least 30 minutes of moderate activity. If you struggle with physical limitations, ask your doctor what might help you or seek guidance from a physical therapist or exercise physiologist. Sometimes when one part of the body is struggling, there are other parts that we can move and exercise.

> ➤ No naps – a brief nap can be refreshing and is not bad for us. It shouldn't last longer than 20 minutes. More than that, and later in the day, a nap can impede the sleep process (Pacheco and Wright, 2020).
> *You can get more information from the Sleep Foundation.

To recap, sleep hygiene is having good sleep habits that help you get restful sleep. In clarifying some of the sleep hygiene strategies, I mentioned a couple things I want to go into even more detail on.

REM Sleep Highlight

What is REM Sleep? REM stands for Rapid Eye Movement. REM Sleep is considered the most restorative for the brain and body. During REM sleep our brain is almost as active as when we are awake. During this phase researchers believe REM sleep help consolidate memories, it aids in learning, mood, and brain/body recovery. During REM sleep, our breathing can become irregular, but returns to normal as we shift into different phases. Most dreams occur during REM sleep.

> ➤ Lack of REM sleep can reduce coping skills and response to threatening situations.
> ➤ Lack of REM sleep has been linked to migraines.
> ➤ Drinking alcohol reduces REM sleep.

Bedroom Setup

Bedroom setup is one topic because it can influence your ability to sleep. I mentioned the dark room, but also make sure some light comes in. This is where I want to go into more detail because I know some people get the blackout curtains, and then comment that they struggle to wake up. Well, there is a reason for that.

Our bodies are programmed to sync up with the sun. Our bodies produce melatonin when the sun goes down, which promotes sleep, and then reduces as the sun comes up. When sunlight comes in our room our retinas are affected. The retinas in our eyes have light-sensitive cells called photoreceptors that tell the brain whether it's daytime or nighttime and thus affects our sleep cycle. There is much more to the science, but the point here is. Try to get your room dark at night, and if you wake in the middle of the night to go to the bathroom, use a dimmed light to see, rather than the bright bathroom light. But allowing a little natural light to come into the room will help you wake more naturally.

Electronics and Sleep

The next topic to go into even more detail is the concept of electronics. I mentioned a lot above about electronics and if you have them, to listen only. Well, there is a reason for that. The brains' ability to "pay attention" is not a default process and does not allow for multitasking for "attention" related activities (Brain Rules, 2014). I do want to clarify, it is best to learn how to fall asleep and re-fall asleep in the middle of the night or after a 2am bathroom break, without the aid of tools.

The goal should be to find which tools work for you now so that you get your body back to a more natural circadian rhythm, and then slowly reduce or remove the tools to fall asleep naturally.

One of the pitfalls of using tv, podcasts, sound machines is that once you fall asleep, these tools that helped may also be the thing that wakes you up in the middle of the night. Play around to see if the tv or podcast have timers and will shut off, same with sound machine. And make sure they aren't casting light that could be keeping you awake.

To determine what works, select one tool and try it for ten days. Document your sleep. And then try another skill.

Medication and Sleep

Medication question: should I take a medication to sleep? Answer, I can't tell you what is best for you. I'm not that kind of doctor.

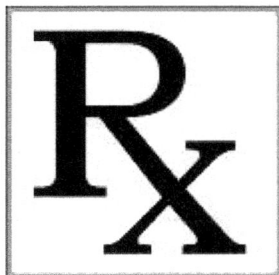

What I would say is, talk to your doctor about all non-medication options first. For some people weaning off medication is very difficult causing significant loss of sleep while the body adjusts to falling asleep without the medication. Conversely, not all herbal or natural remedies work for everyone as well.

Your sleep troubles are specific to you, get specific help.

Which goes back to my belief, a health checkup with your primary care doctor is something to do each year. I love America; however, it is built into our culture to push through and ignore things until you can't ignore them anymore. I don't agree with that. I'm proactive and believe in a yearly checkup for preventative care.

If you are struggling with sleep, talk to your doctor, make sure there is nothing physical going on, try different tools, and talk to a therapist if there is something emotional
or cognitive/stressful going on.

Sleep Journal
Exercise:

Let's pay attention for one week, keep a sleep journal. Write down what is going on when you go to sleep and how well you sleep.

Date/Time	How are you feeling overall?	How was the quality of sleep?	Notes

Date/Time	How are you feeling overall?	How was the quality of sleep?	Notes

Date/Time	How are you feeling overall?	How was the quality of sleep?	Notes

Date/Time	How are you feeling overall?	How was the quality of sleep?	Notes

Chapter Twelve – Investing in Your Life

This chapter is the last of the workbook and is one of the most important chapters. It is about creating your authentic self. Hopefully you have participated in the exercises in cognitive distortions, understanding feelings and emotions, getting to know your worldview, you are hopefully learning to set boundaries, develop your self-worth, embrace the word and, you are practicing mindfulness, using positive coping skills, paying attention to your nutrition and exercise, learning how to get good sleep, but now it is time to pull it all together and solidify your identity.

what is self-identity?

The Oxford Dictionary refers to it as the recognition of one's potential and qualities as an individual. What does that mean. It is belief in your self-worth, it is having pride in yourself (different than being prideful), and it is knowing your values. It doesn't take much, but the little it takes is important.

What do you need to know?

> ➢ You need to know your values,
> ➢ you need to know your skills and/or talents,
> ➢ you need to know your likes and dislikes,
> ➢ and you need to know those little qualities that make you; YOU!

Let's break them down.

Knowing Your Values

I'm going to list a few values just to get you started, but you can search for more value words. There are easily a 100 value words out there. I've listed some words that you should hopefully know the definition of. And if you aren't sure, look them up.

Let me give you an example of why it is important to look them up and confirm your understanding.

Wrong Definitions

I ask people all the time, what is the definition of "failure."

Many people will say, "well, failing at something" or "not doing something right" or even "didn't finish". Those are part of the definition, and something to note.

Did you hear the judgment is those definitions? Now you can look at a few dictionaries and the definition will change, but basically the definition is **"not completing a goal"**. It's very close to the others isn't it, but hopefully you see the one difference. There is no judgement. Just a fact. "didn't complete a goal."

And ultimately it is not a terrible thing to fail, to not complete a goal. We are human, we will fail. That is how we learn.

It just means we might be missing information, training, or skill to complete the goal. And if we get that missing bit of information, if we try again, possibly we will "attain the goal" or have success.

Going back to the value words. If you are not sure you know the true value words, then look them up. In fact, with online systems you can look up these words and get the definition from two or three sources just to see the most common definition.

You might have fun looking up these words:
- ➢ Success
- ➢ Achievement
- ➢ Perfection
- ➢ Martyr
- ➢ Truth
- ➢ Perspective

Values Exercise:

Here is your beginning; which are your top 5 values? You can list value words from other sources as well. We did this in Part 2, Chapter 4, but lets review.

Accountability	Achievement	Adaptability
Appreciation	Authenticity	Balance
Community	Compassion	Courage
Creativity	Forgiveness	Freedom
Generosity	Growth	Integrity
Justice	Kindness	Learning
Listening	Love	Loyalty
Openness	Patience	Prudence
Reciprocity	Respect	Resilience
Self-Compassion	Self-giving	Vision

1. _____

2. _____

3. _____

4. _____

5. _____

Make sure every day you ask yourself; "Am I focused on at least one of my values today." Get to know your values. They may be different from your friends, family, and coworkers, and that is okay. You were all raised differently, in different decades, maybe in different locations, with different world events going on. We are better because we are a bit different.

Knowing Your Skills and/or Talents

Yes, we all have at least a couple skills or talents. The struggle here is, for many people if it isn't spectacular, it isn't special. That is not correct. All talents and/or skills are special, even if everyone can do it and even if no one cares. This is about you being excited for your own abilities.

A skill or talent can be your special personality, your ability to give positive words, your acceptance of others, compassion, coaching, your communication skills, your resilience, or even your determination.

It may be hard to think of your "everyday self" as having something extra special, but I'm sure you do. If it helps, start with the ways you are different from your friends or family.

List your skills or talents:

1. _____

2. _____

3. _____

4. _____

5. _____

Knowing Your Likes and Dislikes

Just like knowing our values and our skills/talents, it is equally important to know our likes and dislikes. Likes and dislikes can be tangible (mani/pedi, massage, dogs, cars, etc.) or intangible (values, spirituality, holidays, etc.).

It is normal to struggle with this area. Over the years I have talked with people who can list one or the other (likes or dislikes), but struggle with both. In fact, this may take a week or two to complete because you need to be "reminded" of what you like or dislike.

Now let's clarify, when I say like or dislike, I don't just mean chocolate or a beer. I mean that you like it so much that if someone asked you to never do it/engage in it again it would be devastating. And for a dislike, that if someone did this or you experienced this, daily or weekly, it would be disruptive in your life. I hope that makes sense.

If it helps, go back to the chapter on **boundaries**.

Likes:

1. _____

2. _____

3. _____

4. _____

5. _____

6. _____

7. _____

8. _____

9. _____

10. _____

Dislikes:

1. _____

2. _____

3. _____

4. _____

5. _____

6. _____

7. _____

8. _____

9. _____

10. _____

Knowing Those Qualities That Make You; You

I hope your self-identity is starting to become clearer. You now know your values, your skills and/or talents, and your likes and dislikes. Let's start working on the qualities that make you; you.

This can be really anything. For example, one of my "fun fantasies," which is actually a possibility, is for me to own and run a "goofy golf" in my retirement years. I used to go to one is Fort Walton Beach, Florida as a child, adolescent, teen, young adult; well, you get the point. I love this place. Its inexpensive, it's fun, and it's a great break for a couple hours. I love arts and crafts and being outside. I would love to retire and own one. Most of my family and friends can say they have never met anyone who wants to own a goofy golf. That is a quality that makes me; me.

It is the little things, anything, it is the combination of stuff that we love, that we have passions for, that we value, etc. that make us who we are.

Can you list 5 things that make you: YOU?

1. _____

2. _____

3. _____

4. _____

5. _____

Are there areas that you aren't sure about? That is okay. In fact, that is great. Why, because that is the whole point of "investing in your life."

You now get an opportunity to learn even more about yourself. Take the time to investigate something new. Trying a new restaurant, or a new meal at the same restaurant is great. Try a new movie theater, or a new park to walk. Visit a new town. One of my favorite towns is an hour drive from my home and it has the best little beach restaurant. A four-hour drive from my home, and crossing a state line, is a place where you can take a train ride.

Taking the time to try new things (food, clothing, adventures, movies, books, etc.) are ways to see how you have grown and changed over time. The most important thing, make sure you love something because you love it, not because everyone else does or doesn't around you. The more comfortable you are with you, even with being different from your friends or family, the less worrisome you may feel. Accepting yourself, for all your values, skills, talents, likes and dislikes, and those qualities that make you; you; are a part of what brings calm into your life.

It doesn't mean that life won't bring some ups and downs your way, but it does mean during those unpleasant times that you are still grounded in who you are.

Self-Discovery Exercise:

List those things that you are not sure about, so you can make plans to try something new.

I personally love festival season, it's a great time to try new foods and events.

1. _____
2. _____
3. _____
4. _____
5. _____
6. _____
7. _____
8. _____
9. _____
10. _____
11. _____
12. _____

Afterword: When Self-Help is Not Enough

I've said this several times throughout this book, if you need additional help, seek it. This book is only general information and is not specific to any one person's situation. In fact, as much as I love self-help books, they can't be anything more than general.

This book is geared to help people gain self-confidence, learn themselves, and learn healthy lifestyle tips which may help reduce worry and anxious moments. Or it may help you identify an issue so that you aren't calling it anxiety and instead you are seeing the specialized help.

There are varieties of health professionals who specialize in psychology, nutrition, physical rehab, and medical ailments. Go see them if you aren't feeling well for a consistent period of time.

What is a consistent period of time, that I can't say, again, it is subjective to each person's need. But I would say, if you have doubts, go see a professional because now at least you aren't guessing if there is something wrong with you. I can say, there is nothing worse than guessing.

I hope at the end of this book, what you have learned are different strategies to embrace and increase a health and wellness lifestyle. And that you have stopped using the word Anxiety. While feeling anxious is a valid feeling, anxiety is a dead end. Create movement in your life. Start using specific feeling words to describe your worries. And if it is hard, which I know it can be. Seek a therapist who is specifically trained in Anxiety and allow them to help you create change.

References:

American Psychiatric Association, The (2013). Diagnostic and statistical manual of mental disorders (5th ed.). Arlington, VA: American Psychiatric Publishing.

Bigsby, E., Cappella, J. N., & Seitz, H. H. (2013). Efficiently and effectively evaluating public service announcements: Additional evidence for the utility of perceived effectiveness. *Communication Monographs, 80*(1), 1–23. doi:10.1080/03637751.2012.739706

Brown, T. C., Fry, M. D., & Little, T. D. (2013). The psychometric properties of the perceived motivational climate in exercise questionnaire. *Measurement in Physical Education and Exercise Science, 17*(1), 22–39. doi:10.1080/1091367X.2013.741360

CDC, 2016. Tips for Better Sleep. Sleep and Sleep Disorders. https://www.cdc.gov/sleep/about_sleep/sleep_hygiene.html

Choi, J. H., Chung, K., & Park, K. (2013). Psychosocial predictors of four health-promoting behaviors for cancer prevention using the stage of change of transtheoretical model. *Psycho-Oncology, 22*, 2253–2261.

Conner, M., McEachan, R., Lawton, R., & Gardner, P. (2016). Basis of intentions as a moderator of the intention–health behavior relationship. *Health Psychology, 35*, 219–227. doi:10.1037/hea0000261

Contrada, R. J. (2011). *Stress, adaptation, and health.* In R. J. Contrada & Baum (Eds.), The handbook of stress science: Biology, psychology, and health (pp. 1–9). New York, NY: Springer Publishing Company.

Erickson, J. (2018). Public Service Announcements to Promote
Physical Activity. *Walden Dissertations and Doctoral Studies.*
5621. https://scholarworks.waldenu.edu/dissertations/5621

Esposito, G., van Bavel, R., Baranowski, T., & Duch-Brown, N.
(2016). Applying the model of goal-directed behavior,
including descriptive norms, to physical activity intentions: A
contribution to improving the theory of planned behavior.
Psychological Reports, 119(1), 5–26.
doi:10.1177/0033294116649576

Glanz, K., Rimer, B. K., & Viswanath, K. (Eds.). (2008). *Health
behavior and health education: Theory, research, and practice*
(4th ed.). San Francisco, CA: Jossey- Bass.

Goleman, D. Personality: Major Traits Found Stable Throughout
Life. *The New York Times.* Published June 9, 1987.

Grappone, G. (2018). Overcoming Stigma. *National Alliance on
Mental Illness.* Overcoming Stigma | NAMI: National
Alliance on Mental Illness

Haug, J. (2013). The 'Diversity' Movement: Defeating Itself,
Destroying Society. *The American Thinker.* The 'Diversity'
Movement: Defeating Itself, Destroying Society - American
Thinker

Hobbs, N., Dixon, D., Johnston, M., & Howie, K. (2013). Can the
theory of planned behaviour predict the physical activity
behaviour of individuals? *Psychology & Health, 28*, 234–249.
doi:10.1080/08870446.2012.716838

Institutes of Health. (n.d.). *Consumer health informatics research
resources; behavioral intention.* Retrieved from
https://chirr.nlm.nih.gov/behavioral-intention.php

King University Online. (2021). What Does a Health Psychologist Do? | King University Online.

Lienemann, B. A., Siegel, J. T., & Crano, W. D. (2013). Persuading people with depression to seek help: Respect the boomerang. *Health Communication, 28*, 718–728. doi:10.1080/10410236.2012.712091

Medina, J. (2014). 12 Principles for Surviving and Thriving at Work, Home, and School. *Brain Rules*; Audio Book by Libro.fm.

Pacheco, D. & Wright, H. (2020). Does Napping During the Day Affect Your Sleep at Night? Sleep Foundation. Does Napping Impact Sleep at Night? | Sleep Foundation

Payne, Beth. (2020). What Resilience is Not. Payne Resilience Training & Consulting. What Resilience is Not — Payne Resilience Training & Consulting

Pittman, C. M. & Karle, E. M. (2015). Rewire Your Anxious Brain: How to Use the Neuroscience of Fear to End Anxiety, Panic, and Worry. Oakland, CA: New Harbinger.

Rhodes, R. E., & Dickau, L. (2013). Moderators of the intention-behaviour relationship in the physical activity domain: A systematic review. *British Journal of Sports Medicine, 47*, 215–225. doi:10.1136/bjsports-2011-090411

Roberts, B. W., & Mroczek, D. (2008). Personality Trait Change in Adulthood. *Current directions in psychological science, 17*(1), 31–35. https://doi.org/10.1111/j.1467-8721.2008.00543.x

Sleep Foundation. (2021). Sleep Deprivation. *Sleep Foundation.* https://www.sleepfoundation.org/sleep-deprivation

Steimer T. (2002). The biology of fear- and anxiety-related
behaviors. *Dialogues in clinical neuroscience*, *4*(3), 231–249.
https://doi.org/10.31887/DCNS.2002.4.3/tsteimer

van der Kaap-Deeder, J., Vansteenkiste, M., Soenens, B., Verstuyf,
J., Boone, L., & Smets, J. (2014). Fostering self-endorsed
motivation to change in patients with an eating disorder: The
role of perceived autonomy support and psychological need
satisfaction. *International Journal of Eating Disorders, 47*,
585–600. doi:10.1002/eat.22266

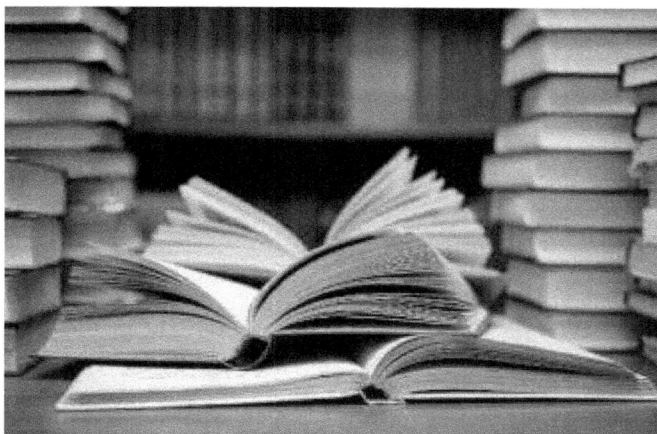

About The Author

I started writing short stories when I was a young child. I loved creating an adventure for myself. Along with that, I started taking pictures before I was in middle school.

Now, I enjoy combining my two favorite hobbies with my career. I get to write workbooks or self-help books on my favorite topic; Anxiety (or really recovery from it). Many of the pictures in my books are pictures I've taken.

Anxiety a topic I became familiar with when I was in my early 20's. I was in my first professional job, I was married, had two young children, trying to advance professionally, and I worked in Healthcare, where employees tend to be anxious just due to the nature of what we all do.

Out of 20+ years in Healthcare Administration, I spent 17 of it in management or supervisory roles. While dealing with personnel issues does get old, I never stopped loving the corporate atmosphere, the projects, and the deadlines.

After I hit the 20-year mark though, I did realize I wanted a change. It was either up the corporate ladder, or something different. So, I went the route of something different.

I went back to school, got my master's in counseling, and kept going. I received my Ph.D. in Health Psychology in 2018, from Walden University. My dissertation focused on using video public service announcements to motivate people to engage in physical activity.
Promoting personal empowerment to make positive change is something that I strive for, and really enjoy helping other strive for that as well.

Helping younger professionals find their confidence, find their voice, and find their place in a room filled with people more in my age group is also a passion of mine.

In 2016 I completed a study abroad for 4 months to further my cultural understandings and honestly, I wanted to get away for a bit. I lived in Ireland and traveled around western Europe for four months. The best time of my life.

When I'm not working as a psychologist, I enjoy traveling, writing, and taking pictures.

If you would like to read my article about motivating people to engage in physical activity via video Public Service Announcements, it has been published in the Journal of Social, Behavioral, and Health Sciences.

My favorite quote by Robert Frost
~ **Two roads diverged in a wood, and I, I took the one less traveled by, and that has made all the difference.**

www.ingramcontent.com/pod-product-compliance
Lightning Source LLC
Chambersburg PA
CBHW060039030426
42334CB00019B/2405